D.R. Wilha—
Byrmaon
Ghristma— 1988

Towards
a Civilisation
of Love

14/46.

Towards a Civilisation of Love

Being Church in Today's World

Cardinal Basil Hume

Hodder & Stoughton
LONDON SYDNEY AUCKLAND TORONTO

Bible quotations are taken from the
Revised Standard Version.

British Library Cataloguing in Publication Data

Hume, Basil, *1923–*
  Towards a civilisation of love.
  1. Society. Role of Catholic Church
  I. Title
  282

  ISBN 0-340-48936-7 Hbk
  ISBN 0-340-48931-6 Pbk

First published 1988

Printed in Great Britain for Hodder and Stoughton Ltd., Mill Road, Dunton Green,
Sevenoaks, Kent by St Edmundsbury Press Ltd., Bury St Edmunds, Suffolk.

Photoset by Rowland Phototypesetting Ltd., Bury St Edmunds, Suffolk.

Hodder and Stoughton Editorial Office: 47 Bedford Square, London, WC1B 3DP.

The Church today is faced with an immense task: to humanise and to Christianise this modern civilisation of ours. The continued development of this civilisation, indeed its very survival, demand and insist that the Church do her part in the world.

John XXIII, Mater et Magistra, May 15th, 1961

We are called to be physicians of that civilisation about which we dream, the civilisation of love.

Paul VI, December 31st, 1975

Peace can write the finest pages of history, inscribing them not only with the magnificence of power and glory but also with the greater magnificence of human virtue, people's goodness, collective prosperity and true civilisation: the civilisation of love.

Paul VI, Peace Day Message, January 1977

Contents

Preface

I was invited to give a number of talks in Australia in January 1988. The occasions were important ones and I knew that the talks would have to be carefully prepared. That was not easy. I have then to acknowledge that without the help of Monsignor George Leonard the work would never have been completed. I benefited too from the assistance of Monsignor Vincent Nichols and Father John Arnold. We spent considerable time together reflecting on the contribution of the Second Vatican Council to our understanding of the Church. We took into account also the Extraordinary Synod of 1985 and the Synod on the role and mission of the laity in 1987, together with the results of extensive national consultation which preceded both of these.

This book was prepared for publication before the Holy Father completed the 1987 Synod with his official and authoritative contribution. Inevitably it is limited in scope. There is so much more that could be said about the Church, the sacraments, Christian unity and much else. I am also aware that I have not written explicitly about priesthood and religious life. The laity will, I trust, play an increasingly important part in the mission of the Church, but that will always be in close collaboration with priests and religious. The preaching of the Word, the celebration of Mass and the administration of the sacraments – these are at the heart of the Church's life and mission. They cannot be without our priests.

As a mark of respect and gratitude I dedicate this book to all of them.

June 1988   BASIL HUME

Acknowledgments

Chapters 2, 3, 4, 5, 7, 10 are based on lectures given in Hobart and Melbourne, Australia, and St Louis, Missouri, USA, in January and February 1988.

Chapter 11 is an edited version of a lecture given to a Christianne Brusselman's Seminar in Bruges, Belgium in June 1985 and first published in *Briefing*, vol. 15, no. 13.

Chapter 9 was in large part given as a lecture in All Hallows College, Dublin in September 1986 and published in its original form in the *Furrow*, November 1986, under the title 'Europe, the Church and the Synod'.

1

In the Fullness of Time

But when the time had fully come, God sent forth his Son,
born of woman, born under the law. *Galatians 4:4*

To those who saw him in the flesh Jesus Christ remained an
enigma. He taught obliquely in homely stories that concealed
as much as they revealed. He explained to his disciples: 'This
is why I speak to them in parables, because seeing they do not
see, and hearing they do not hear, nor do they understand'
(Matt. 13:13). Slowly they were led to realise that they had to
enter a new dimension where the physical and material would
reveal to the eyes of faith a further reality which is eternal and
transcendent. In this new creation nothing is simply what it
seems. Experience beckons us on into mystery, into the heart
of all that is.

It should come then as no surprise to discover that there is
much more in the Church of Jesus Christ than meets the eye
or can be measured in purely human terms. Nobody can be
unaware of the immense tangible presence of the Church
throughout two millennia of Christian history. Cathedrals
and parish churches are a constant and distinctive feature of
our towns and cities and witness to a faith that has shaped the
past and present. Popes and prelates, thinkers and poets,
saints and reformers have left their mark on society and
human affairs. Schools, charitable organisations and religious
orders have cared for the needs of people for centuries. Yet

the secret energy of the Church, its inner identity, is not to be found in its structures nor in anything measurable. The true nature of the Church escapes our unaided observation and can be glimpsed only by faith. Once again we are in the realm of mystery. The Church is incapable of final analysis because its inmost reality is so overwhelming. Yet it has a name. It is Emmanuel which means God is with us. Jesus Christ lives now and always and is in our midst. We encounter him in a special way whenever we are involved in and with the Church.

There is no institution as familiar and yet as mysterious as the Church. No achievement of the human spirit, no expression of human solidarity is more prized and yet still so imperfectly understood. I am convinced that an ever-deepening knowledge of the Church holds the answer to some of life's most significant questions. It affords us entry into the promised land where we can encounter God in daily life and explore something of his infinite beauty and goodness and truth while still this side of eternity.

Whenever we speak and think about God and about his particular presence among us in the Church, we have to resort to images of life and growth or search. Our Lord spoke of the Spirit who would lead us into all truth. The emphasis is always on pilgrimage and discovery. When Christians are baptised into Christ they are initiated into a life which, like an eternal spring, never ceases to pour out of the rock which is Christ. Faith, which is God's gift to us in baptism, remains incomplete, ever thirsting for fulfilment. Baptism points forward to Eucharist and Eucharist to the eternal banquet in the everlasting kingdom. All our images and concepts of the Church are essentially partial, prophetic. In the here and now we yearn for the 'not yet'. We live with imperfection and impermanence.

Given to the world as a sacrament, an effective symbol of God's life and love, the Church has so often experienced conflict and dissent. Although now entering an exciting era of renewal and reconciliation, the Church will tread the way of the cross in its search for organic reunion, for experienced wholeness. In my vision of what lies ahead for the Church in the decades ahead I see Calvary rather than the Easter garden. The cross will have to be embraced and loved as the symbol and effective means of our encounter with God. The Christian Church is not entering into a period of light and ease. The night of unbelief will grow still darker before the dawn. The forces of good and evil are locked in a battle that will endure to the end of time. Christ has won the decisive victory but the warfare continues, each generation taking its share of struggle, danger and pain. Christ, triumphant over death and sin, bears in his body the marks of the nails and the spear-thrust. Christian unity, so significant an element in the mission and ministry of the Church, will be achieved slowly, painfully and at great cost. I foresee a period of much agonised prayer, difficult dialogue and inevitable disappoint- ments. Yet there must also be an inner assurance that the struggle and the daily deaths necessary in the search for unity are of God and lead to resurrection.

That resurrection must of necessity be a new creation. It cannot be a turning back of the clock to the era of the undivided Church, a millennium ago. The renewed and reunited Church will be the work of the Holy Spirit, fashioned in the turbulence and flame of a perennial Pentecost. But only the eyes of faith will see it for what it truly is. In some way presently irreconcilable views will have to be reconciled and Christian communities will have to learn to grow together in faith. There are no short cuts, there is no magic formula.

In the wake of Pope John Paul II's visit to Britain in 1982 some thought that reunion was within our grasp. Frustration quickly followed. I am convinced that the slow, almost imper- ceptible, organic growth of unity will demand of us all two basic qualities in the years ahead. We shall need an immense unshakeable trust in God. The work for Christian unity is of God and cannot ultimately be frustrated or denied. It is true that we must work and pray for it and not simply wait for it, but we do so with quiet assurance and confidence in each other. At all times there is need for courage and a stout heart. It is more common to take refuge in despair and to seek the security of the familiar and the seemingly safe; it takes bravery to accept vulnerability and apparent failure.

Two words constantly suggest themselves to my mind when reflecting on Christian unity. They are gift and growth. Christian unity is in no way a human achievement but is a gift of God's love and a sharing in his life. It is, in the most obvious sense, a grace, undeserved and humanly unattainable. We pray for it, welcome it, clear away obstacles to it, give thanks for it, respond effectively to it. But at all times we recognise that it is not the product of human ingenuity or of ecclesiastical politics but is freely given by God and fruit of that constant conversion of mind and heart which is at the root of all Christian living and is also gift.

Growth is inherent in any vital process. We do not make progress in the life of Christ's body by leaps and bounds, by changes effected in the twinkling of an eye. Separated Christian communities have a life of their own, a sense of their own identity and history, an individual approach to Christian revelation and tradition. To heal the wounds of division, to come together in freedom and love requires a certain maturing, an openness to growth and development and, above all, time for the process to happen. There is a certain impatience which claims for itself religious zeal but which can, and often does, assume that the one thing necessary is effort. Patience in face of the imperceptible is sometimes a necessary virtue.

Emphasis on the difficulties of Christian unity can overlook the very real dissension that can exist within a Church that believes itself already to be reconciled. The ideal of a Christian community devoted like the first group of believers in Jerusalem 'to the apostles' teaching and fellowship, to the breaking of bread and the prayers' (Acts 2:42) is sometimes more honoured in the breach than in the observance. Yet any vision which embraces being Church in today's world must take stock of the diversity which persists within the unity and inhibits its growth.

There can be a divergence of approach and emphasis within a community that is entirely healthy, normal and creative. There can also arise dissension which is destructive and divisive. Within the Catholic community, for instance, there is an entirely legitimate divergence on many issues of justice, Third World development, war and peace. At the same time there certainly exists dissension on matters which touch directly on the source of authority within the Church and the acceptance of legitimately sanctioned liturgical reforms. Here the dissension often results in a refusal to worship together and to receive Holy Communion at the same Mass. It is tragically possible that this state of virtual schism could become a conscious secession with all its painful consequences. There is nothing more damaging to the Church than schism, nothing more insidious than those who in claiming to be Catholic stand apart from the Pope and the bishops.

Dissension is no new phenomenon among believers. Christian history bears witness to it and its effects have become institutionalised. In present times, however, conflict and disunity have added impact because of immensely improved communications. A local or national protest can easily be flashed around the world and become the focus of international attention in a matter of hours. This heightens the level of tension under which we all live and encourages dissidents to seek ways of dramatising their contentions. Inevitably this diminishes the joy and certainty that people have in their faith and soaks up energy which could have been put to better use in other spheres of Christian witness and concern.

This is not unimportant as we enter the final years of this millennium. I do not know if it is merely coincidental or self-induced but, as we consciously prepare for the third millennium, there is in the air undoubtedly a sense of expectation and perhaps even of a certain climax. Events seem to be moving towards some kind of denouement, a new and perhaps decisive epoch in history. The Church as always has to be ready to meet the spiritual and moral needs of this age.

Already the final decade of the second millennium is being seen as a period for renewed and sustained evangelisation, the bringing of the perennial Gospel to the contemporary world. Pope John Paul II has set aside 1987–8 as Marian Year. It is his intention that deeper devotion to the Mother of Christ and Mother of the Church should preface renewed dedication both to Christ himself and to his Church.

In January 1986 he had urged the bishops of Europe to undertake afresh the evangelising of their ancient continent. Increasingly it has become obvious that the age of enlightenment is now psychologically and morally bankrupt. The underlying consensus on values which had held society together no longer exists in any effective way. There is now both need and opportunity for the Gospel once again to fill the spiritual void. The Church will have to bring to the contemporary world a more vivid awareness of God's life and love.

As it faces this task, the Church of the 1990s is markedly different in appearance and approach from that of the mid-century. Nowhere is this more evident than in the role and ministry of the papacy. Theologically and juridically nothing has changed but in the past decade Pope John Paul II has built on the achievements of his four immediate predecessors to transform all hitherto accepted notions of how to be bishop of Rome and successor of Peter. The theological insights of Pius XII, the humanity and trustfulness of John XXIII, the pastoral and intellectual coherence of Paul VI, the fleeting smile of John Paul I, made possible the breakthrough effected by the present Pope with such flair and energy. He has harnessed today's technology in the service of the Gospel.

His pastoral visits worldwide have a twofold purpose. They bring the successor of Peter to each local church so that he might confirm the faith of his brethren and make visible the bonds of unity between them. They also make it possible for him to fulfil the role of universal evangelist. He is able to proclaim the Gospel and uphold its values even in situations of great difficulty.

The more I am involved in the affairs of the Church the more I appreciate the role of Peter's successor to represent in his office and person that unity of faith and charity so essential to the life of the Church. The papacy for today's world offers the possibility of dialogue and reconciliation. This was strikingly illustrated for me in October 1986 when the Pope brought together in Assisi the leaders of the Christian churches and the world religions to pray for world peace. My imagination is still fired by the symbol of Pope John Paul in St Mary of the Angels in the midst of other Christians from East and West, and in the piazza outside the basilica of St Francis, flanked by those of other faiths who represent the religious instinct of today's world. It opened up for me an understanding of how the papacy might unite the forces of faith in the service of the world's most pressing needs. I found this particularly affecting since, but a few days before, I had stood amidst the desolation and despair of Auschwitz during an assembly in Poland of Europe's Catholic bishops. Auschwitz represents for me the ultimate degradation of fallen humanity. It is a stark monument to an evil philosophy which sought to reduce to nothing, literally to annihilate, the Jewish people that gave birth to Jesus Christ. From war and bestial cruelty to peace and all-embracing love, from the ruins of human vainglory to the building of a new civilisation, today's world is being called to turn its back on the failures of the past and to look to the future with faith and hope. In this task the papacy is no longer the obstacle to world unity as Paul VI feared, but is perhaps the necessary bridge across which churches and religions might cross to find common ground. Prophetically the pope from earliest times has claimed the title Bridge-builder, Pontifex. Only in our time have the cosmic possibilities of this role begun to be adequately explored.

The renewal of the papacy is just one aspect of the reawakening of the Church in our day, a process which, historically, entered a new and decisive phase with the Second Vatican Council. Many express disappointment at what they see as the frustration of their high hopes of the Council's reforms. Others bemoan what they experience as the collapse of certainty following the Council. What they all ignore is the evidence before their eyes of the growth in life and love of the Church in recent years. It is all too easy to forget the point of departure, to fail to measure the distance already covered in the pilgrim way. Despite the occasional failures and setbacks in any human endeavour, the Church of today provides proof of a more profound self-understanding and a renewed vitality. It demonstrates in new and sometimes surprising ways what it means in contemporary terms to be one, holy, catholic and apostolic.

I have already indicated how the Church today seeks unity not only within itself but with other Christians and believers. But that unity is only the seed and symbol of a unity in which all diversity is ultimately to be reconciled. The Second Vatican Council described the Church as 'a sign and instrument of communion with God and of unity among all men' (Lumen Gentium 1). The whole human race, created in the image and likeness of God, patterned on the Word 'in whom all things were made', is to be brought to its destined unity in Christ and thereby to be made partaker of divine life and love in this world and hereafter. That ultimately is the vision of the Church of Christ in its fullness where Christ is all and is in all. It transcends time and place, embraces all nations, encompasses all history. It may be hard to equate this vision of global reconciliation with the reality of the institutional Church past and present. All too often pastors and people have clung to a concept of the Church that is exclusive, domineering and triumphalist. Even evangelism has sometimes in the past seemed associated with a kind of cultural and religious imperialism. True to itself the Church has, however, to respect each individual's particular worth and dignity and to create unity without loss of legitimate diversity. Only in the life and love of the Triune God is such a process possible and it can reach perfection only in eternity.

The new awareness of, and yearning for, holiness is another aspect of being Church in today's world which is rooted in the perennial life of the Church but which now rejoices in new vigour and wholeness. Today a spirituality is emerging which is total in that it is a way of life which is open to all and which embraces every activity in life. There is now seen to be no dichotomy between religion and life, the sacred and the secular, and so goodness and justice, commitment and compassion are inseparable. A Church is coming to life, all of whose members are seen to be called equally to lives of holiness, truth and love. Already in that Church new forms of association and service are springing up. There is fresh interest in prayer and evidence of a thirst for the things of the spirit. The flourishing retreat movement, the growth of prayer groups, the wider distribution of devotional and religious literature all confirm this trend. Its importance cannot be overestimated; its characteristics are worth closer study.

Today in a special way the Church is becoming conscious also of the deeper implications of its catholicity. As Henri de Lubac wrote:

She accepts no frontier, either geographical or social, as a check to her expansion; she does not stop short even at the frontier of the visible world, for, in accordance with a terminology long traditional, she is distinguished into three groups in ceaseless inter-communication – the Church Militant in this world, the Church Suffering in purgatory and the Church Triumphant (although the triumph is not yet complete, since it awaits the day of days when the Church will be totally victorious after the glorious coming of her Saviour). (*The Splendour of the Church*, p. 30)

De Lubac points out that the real believer is never therefore alone in his or her faith. Solidarity with his brothers and sisters in Christ remains a source of comfort and strength: 'The richness of the thing is unique; nothing comparable has ever been thought up by men, let alone realised. If, for example, one were to speak of a Buddhist or a Taoist church, it could only be in virtue of a very distant analogy. And this richness is marvellously multiform' (ibid. p. 31).

Although the ideal of catholicity has been enshrined from the beginning in the concept of Church, only in recent years has it become a lived reality. It is not just a matter of solidarity between all races in the one fellowship, it is also a matter of genuine equality of respect and responsibility between male and female to match their equal baptismal grace and calling. In this context I think it significant that this century has been characterised by much reflection on, and rediscovery of, the feminine in God, or, better, by the realisation that the whole of humanity, masculine and feminine, finds its origin and its perfection in God. The catholicity of the Church has been expressed in our time, not only by examples of outstanding holiness in different parts of the world and in different cultures, but by a series of women saints who in different ways have expressed obedience, poverty and joyous delight in God and his creation. I think of Bernadette, the asthmatic visionary of Lourdes, content to be a channel of revelation and, her task completed, to be left in a corner like a broom when the room has been swept. I think of Thérèse of Lisieux, a young contemplative who fashioned 'a little way' of generous abandon and trusting love. Finally I think of that saint of our own day, Mother Teresa of Calcutta. Her passionate concern for each of God's children, however deprived and poor, is a compelling witness to the belief that Christ is encountered in each individual. These three women happen to be religious but in today's world we meet unacknowledged saints, women in every walk of life, who in their lives express something of the tenderness and the power of God's love.

The Church today experiences in a new way what it also means to be catholic in an international sense. No longer culturally European, the Church now expresses its unity and faith in many languages and forms. The Gospel is taking root in diverse cultures and the Church will not in the next millennium make the mistakes made in earlier centuries when, for instance, the Jesuit missions to China and India were compelled to abandon pioneering efforts to divest Christianity of its European appearance and cultural expression. The unity of the Church has nothing in common with the imposition of uniformity. It does not depend on outward similarities but on an inner coherence, a common inheritance of one life and love given by God. The process of inculturation is still in its infancy. Understanding and courage will be needed to let it grow to maturity.

At first sight it might seem difficult to envisage a renewal of apostolicity, yet in our time that has occurred not only in the transformation of the role of the papacy but also in the rediscovery of what it means in the Church to be a bishop and successor of the apostles. Since the Second Vatican Council the bishops of the world have found that their self-understanding has developed and is constantly expressing itself in a collegiality which is as yet not completely understood or accepted.

In this preliminary sketch of the Church there is no need to treat explicitly of matters touched on later. Suffice it to say that in a world increasingly brought together by communication and high-speed travel the collegiality of the Church's bishops, whether formally invoked or informally expressed in more limited fashion, is a necessary dimension of the Church's life and an essential component of all pastoral care. The universal concern each bishop must have for all the churches ensures the survival of some dioceses under crippling pressures. Political, social and ethical problems usually affect a whole nation and need national response from a bishops' conference. Increasingly, as in contemporary

Europe, countries are so interdependent and tend to provide situations demanding solutions at continental level that bishops and their local churches may be powerless without the support and collaboration of conferences at continental or regional level. As I point out later, the International Synod of Bishops, though open to criticism on some counts, is proving a useful forum, articulating pastoral concern and providing the Holy Father with valuable support in his universal ministry.

Understandably, structures are still in the process of development. One obvious problem they face is that, for historical reasons, lines of communication within the Church tend to work vertically and not horizontally. The Holy See and the local church can with reasonable speed communicate effectively with each other. It is not easy to maintain links between bishops' conferences themselves. This is not unimportant since community depends for its health and development on effective communication. We need further to develop structures and modes of procedure which accurately represent the concept and reality they purport to serve. Self-understanding is essential before reform takes shape.

The Church, one, holy, catholic and apostolic, is both visible organism and profound mystery. In our exploration of what it means to be Church in today's world it is necessary to resist the temptation to view the Church in isolation. It does not exist for itself nor by itself. I am convinced that any theology of Church is inadequate and out of focus if it takes insufficient account of a theology of creation and a deeper understanding of the mystery of the Trinity. Christ – who is the inmost reality of the Church – came to save the world and restore all creation to its original unity and wholeness. And no one can begin to answer the question 'Who is Christ?' without plunging into that ultimate mystery which is the life and love of the Three who are One. Attentive contemplation eventually leads to the realisation that all is ultimately one and God is all in all.

The pilgrim in search of the truth which is in fact the reality 'in which we live and move and have our being' needs to meditate, as it were, inch by inch, the cosmic canvas of creation. The Christian understanding is unique although it is rooted in a vision it shares with Jews and Muslims who are, with us, 'children of Abraham's faith'.

The fundamental insight is that creation is good, flows out of God's love, shares his life. The book of Genesis opens with an account of the making of the universe which constantly repeats the words: 'And God saw that it was good.' It was an act of creation carried out at the word of God's command, a significant symbol in light of the prologue to John's Gospel: 'In the beginning was the Word, and the Word was with God, and the Word was God' (John 1:1). Creation then reflects the inmost nature of God the Creator, can never be considered in isolation from him and is itself one and interdependent. It owes all to God and, as fruit of his love, is itself essentially friendly and nurturing.

'Then God said: Let us make man in our image, after our likeness . . . So God created man in his own image, in the image of God he created him; male and female he created them' (Gen. 1:26–27). So humanity is part of that same creative love, but the human mind and heart reveal the presence and image of God in a unique way. God, says the scripture, breathed into man's nostrils the breath of life and man became a living being. The whole human race, in this insight, is essentially a single family; in each is the breath of God's life, the image of his very self. Man and woman were created to know and love him as friend as he walked with them 'in the garden in the cool of the day' (Gen. 3:8).

Sin brought into the world a living death. It did not destroy the essential goodness of life and creation. It introduced division and conflict in the human family. It excluded the whole race from the peace and plenty of paradise. God spoke in many and varied ways and made covenant with his people. The climax of his revelation to the world is to be found in the coming of Christ into our humanity and our history. The incarnation is a divine irrevocable affirmation of human nature. In Christ we see all that a human being might be. He is blessing, reconciliation, transfiguration. In him Infinity accepted limitation, Immortality death, Omnipotence our human frailty. Life and love, pure and obedient, faithful unto death, overcame all that denies life and love and won for the whole human race the blessing and fullness which is to be found, through faith and baptism, in Christ. The death, resurrection and ascension of Christ made possible the new creation, the new heavens and the new earth, when the Holy Spirit again descended, giving birth to new life and making believers other Christs.

The baptised, now one in Christ, will throughout history make real his presence, carry out his ministry, fulfil his mission. They will be known as Christ is known; they will be loved as Christ is loved; they will, in Christ, know and love the God who is. In this they are made sharers in the life and love of God, one with the Father, in the Son, through the Holy Spirit. Humanity which is the mind and heart of creation is thus caught up in the inmost mystery of God. It thus fulfils a divine plan of love and an eternal destiny. This is the ultimate answer to all questions.

The understanding of the Church as the new creation, the new people, is a radical affirmation of creation and humanity. It contradicts contemporary pessimism about the human condition. Thomas Merton in *Conjectures of a Guilty Bystander* writes:

> The Church realises that now she has to help the world to accept itself . . . The gravity of the situation is seen in the fact that Catholic theology has had to plunge into the task of acquiring entirely new perspectives in the space of a generation or two. But the fact that these perspectives are biblical, concrete, existential, thoroughly based on respect for the world and for man in their actuality gives definite hope . . . of bringing to that world the light it needs in an hour of risk and uncertainty. But that light is, as always, the light of the Gospel. What is new in modern theology is not the essential message but our rethinking of it, our rediscovery in it of insights we had lost. These insights provoke in us neither naïve enthusiasms nor petulant slander of the world, but awaken us to the deep truth of man's sinfulness and hardness of heart, overcome by the love of God and by his restoration of the world in Christ. (p. 322)

The purpose I have set myself is to recapture some of this understanding of the Church and to find in this discovery grounds for hope and for affirmation of a humanity that has lost sight of much of its own dignity and meaning. I am conscious as I try to sketch the outlines of this vision that the image of Church may seem light years away from the often humdrum reality of the local parish, its committees, its families, its clergy and Sunday worship. But Peter, James and John were taken by the Lord to Mount Tabor and there he was transfigured in their sight. The everyday familiar appearance of Christ gave way to a brightness like that of the sun. Even his garments became 'white as light' (Matt. 17:1–8). The disciples were overcome with awe at this vision of the glory in whose presence they lived unawares. Which was the shadow, which the substance? It is no bad thing for us to spend time on our Mount Tabor and to glimpse something of the glory of God within.

2

The Church as Communion

The Church since the Second Vatican Council has been engaged in an intense experience of self-discovery. The four great constitutions of the council – on the Church, on the sources of revelation, on the divine liturgy and on the mission of the Church to the modern world – are bringing us an ever-richer understanding of what is meant by Church. We have moved beyond the former emphasis on the visible, the structured, the hierarchical to a sustained meditation on the unfolding mystery, the inner reality of the Church. It is small wonder that we are straining to fashion a new language to express our deepening insights. We are being forced to rely on words from cultures and theologies older and richer than ours. Until we can find adequate English terms we must – with inevitable difficulty – employ Greek and Latin to convey our meaning. The task of finding an adequate vocabulary is an urgent one if the thoughts of the theologians are to become the common property of the People of God.

The Greek word 'koinonia' is now part of the common language of theologians around the world. It represents a reality as old as the Church itself – because it expresses its inmost mystery. It is well known in Orthodox theological writings. It is beginning to find its way into our own Church documents. It is essential to grasp its meaning. It is generally translated into the Latin word 'communio'. This is scarcely enlightening since there is also no equivalent in English for 'communio'. Various terms have been suggested but none has so far gained acceptance, although each, at least in part, suggests some aspect of this concept which derives its origin from New Testament writings. We can glimpse something of its meaning in words like 'partnership', 'shared life', 'joint partaking' and, most of all, 'fellowship' (J. M. Tillard, art. in *One in Christ*, 1986).

I normally translate 'koinonia' as 'communion' despite being fully aware of a certain imprecision. Like many others I first encountered the word 'communion' when as a small boy I prepared for my first Holy Communion. I was told then that when I received Holy Communion, Jesus was within me and I in him. From one point of view these reflections are an attempt to grasp the deeper meaning and further implications of a word which has been for most of us familiar from childhood onwards. The German theologian, Walter Kaspar, has observed that 'although the concept of "communio" is central in the Council texts, the term itself is not strictly fixed in its usage. Besides "communio" the Council uses a series of similar concepts such as "communitas", "societas" etc. The concept of "communio" itself,' he concludes, 'has different levels of meaning. We are thus confronted with an emerging concept.'

Our present concern, then, is to explore together the meaning of this 'emerging concept'. Our aim will be to discern what the concept of koinonia can contribute to our understanding of the theology of the Church and, in particular, to see its relevance to the work for Christian unity.

We are here dealing with another word and concept increasingly alien to the modern mind: that of 'mystery'. Most people today tend to imagine that what is presently inexplicable is no more than a problem that will be resolved sooner or later by the application or development of knowledge. This is a by-product of our immensely successful scientific approach to reality. It is however central to the religious understanding to maintain that there is a reality which does not yield up its secrets to the power of the unaided human intellect although it is not patently contradictory. St Thomas Aquinas maintained: 'He knows God best who knows that whatever he thinks and says falls short of what God truly is' (Opusculum 10, de Causis, Lect. 6).

When we reflect on koinonia we are at the heart of mystery. We are dealing with the ultimate reality of the Church. We can penetrate ever more deeply into the truth that has been revealed; we can never claim to have exhausted its richness or embraced its fullness.

My first conscious encounter in recent years with the word koinonia occurred when it was used by the Anglican Roman Catholic International Commission. The concept is indeed central to much of ARCIC's argumentation and is used to great effect. For the commission, koinonia is 'a relation between persons resulting from their participation in the one and same reality' (ARCIC Final Report, N.5). In this usage it is possible to discern three elements: there is the reality which is being shared, the sharing as an experience and the bond that is created as a result.

By the time twenty years had elapsed from the ending of the Second Vatican Council there was no doubt that the concept of koinonia had taken root in the theological thinking of the universal Church. The Extraordinary Synod of 1985 not only spoke about koinonia but also showed that it was both a useful theological concept and a lived experience of the Church. The Final Report of that synod declared: 'The ecclesiology of communion is a central and fundamental idea in the documents of the Council . . . Since Vatican Council II much has been done to make the Church, as communion, more clearly understood and more concretely translated into living reality.' Then the Report moves into the heart of the matter. Its words are of prime importance:

What does the complex word 'communion' mean? Fundamentally it is a matter of our communion with God through Jesus Christ in his Holy Spirit. This communion exists through the word of God and the sacraments. Baptism is the door and foundation of the Church's communion; the Eucharist is the source of the whole of Christian life and its summit [cf Lumen Gentium 11]. Communio with the Body of Christ in the Eucharist signifies and brings about, or builds up, the intimate union of all the faithful in the Body of Christ which is the Church [cf 1 Cor. 10:16 ff].

So the ecclesiology of communion cannot be reduced to mere questions of organisation or questions concerning mere powers. However, ecclesiological communion is the foundation for order in the Church and especially for the correct relation between unity and pluriformity in the Church.

The crucially important thinking of the Synod's Report can be summed up in this way: the ultimate reality in which the baptised share is the life of the Trinity. The experience of sharing that life is through the word of God and the sacraments and is preeminently to be found in the Eucharist. The bond or tie or relationship which results forms the ecclesial community. Thus the sharing in the life of the Trinity is communion with the Father through Jesus Christ in the Holy Spirit, three persons, one God. This constitutes the inmost mystery of the Church. 'Koinonia' is not an abstraction but a living reality. The Anglican Roman Catholic International Commission has pointed out how experience led to theory and not vice versa. It stated: 'in the early Christian tradition reflection on the experience of koinonia opened the way to the understanding of the mystery of the Church. Although koinonia is never equated with "Church" in the New Testament, it is the term that most aptly expressed the mystery underlying the various New Testament images of the Church' (ARCIC Final Report, N.4).

The experience of sharing in the life of the Trinity through word and sacrament and the sense of one-ness that resulted was lived daily by the early Christian community. It is described in the Acts of the Apostles. We are told that those Jerusalem Christians were 'of one heart and soul' (Acts 4:32) and 'they devoted themselves to the apostles' teaching and fellowship [koinonia], to the breaking of bread and the prayers' (Acts 2:42). The teaching of the apostles, the breaking of bread and prayer were the three fundamental realities shared by those early Christians creating between them a special relationship. Not only were they 'one in heart and soul' but they 'had all things in common' and 'distributed them to all, as any had need' (Acts 2:44–45). The author of Acts is at pains to point out that the community that lived as one was indeed made up of 'all who believed' (cf Acts 4:32; 5:5; 15:16).

This account points to the two focal points of every Christian community, namely the word of God and the Eucharist, which are the means to a more fundamental and vital communion with the blessed Trinity itself.

If then we want to read how that communio is strained to breaking-point we can turn to 1 Corinthians 1:10–31. We see a community proclaiming loyalty to Paul, Apollos, Cephas, Christ. Paul in his anguish cries out: 'Is Christ divided? Was Paul crucified for you? Or were you baptized in the name of Paul?'

There is nothing more at variance with Christ's will that Christians should be one than the prevalence of dissension or parties in the Christian community. Our communion – we have seen – is with God through Jesus Christ in the Holy Spirit. The communion which the baptised have with each other follows from their each being united with the Trinity. The one-ness of the Trinity, with its diversity of persons, is of course the perfect communion/koinonia. It is the prototype of that communion which those made to the image and likeness of God and recreated in Christ, enjoy among themselves.

The scripture basis for this is to be found in the first letter of St John, 1:3: 'that which we have seen and heard we proclaim also to you, so that you may have fellowship with us; and our fellowship is with the Father and with his Son Jesus Christ'.

The prayer of our Lord at the Last Supper, also recorded by John, revealed the same understanding of the fellowship or communion between Father and Son and of ours with each other, even though the word 'koinonia' was not used in the context:

I do not pray for these only, but also for those who believe in me through their word, that they may all be one; even as thou, Father, art in me, and I in thee, that they also may be in us, so that the world may believe that thou hast sent me. The glory which thou hast given me I have given to them, that they may be one even as we are one, I in them and thou

in me . . . so that the world may know that thou hast sent
me and hast loved them even as thou hast loved me. (John
17:20–23)

St John is doing more than recording the will of Christ for his
Church; he makes clear the inherent contradiction of disunity. Made one in Christ we cannot be separated from each
other or be in fundamental conflict without doing violence to
the body of Christ. The analogy of the body is clear in the New
Testament, and it has to imply a living unity. Disunity is
against the essence of the Church. We have to remember at all
times that Christ himself is our unity. Our communion with
the Father is in Christ. This unity embraces a rich diversity of
gifts, an endless blossoming of life. 'Now there are varieties of
gifts, but the same Spirit; and there are varieties of service,
but the same Lord; and there are varieties of working, but it is
the same God who inspires them all in every one' (1 Cor.
12:4–6). The charisms which Paul describes in this same
chapter are intrinsic to the communio. But all is held in the
unity of the triune God. That is the reason why Paul moves
into his often-quoted hymn to love in Chapter 13. It is to be
read in an ecclesial context: it refers not so much to personal
dispositions as to God's love which is the origin and reality of
the unity which is koinonia.

    Through baptism we become part of the people of God and
members, too, of the body of Christ. This image of the body is
but one of a variety used by St Paul to describe how we are
united with Christ and with each other but it remains one of
the clearest and most helpful. We are members of a body
which has Christ as its head. 'He is the head of the body, the
church' (Col. 1:18) and again 'Being many we are one body in
Christ'. Baptism incorporated us into the body of Christ. We
are given new life which we share with all the baptised. St Paul
puts it this way: 'We were buried therefore with him by
baptism into death, so that as Christ was raised from the dead
by the glory of the Father, we too might walk in newness of
life' (Rom. 6:4).

    To enrich further our understanding of koinonia we have to
reflect more deeply on the role of the Holy Spirit. Our
communion with the Father which is in the Son is through the

Holy Spirit. The Spirit brooded over the waters of chaos and the world was brought into being. The Holy Spirit overshadowed the Virgin Mary and so what was born of her was Son of God. In fire and wind the Spirit was poured out over the disciples in the Upper Room and the Church of Christ was born. The Holy Spirit is said by the Council to be 'responsible for the fellowship of the faithful that is so remarkable he gives them a deep attachment to each other in Christ. He is then the principle of the Church's unity' (Decree on Ecumenism, Unitatis Redintegratio, N.2).

The theology of the Orthodox churches has always placed the Holy Spirit at the heart of koinonia. For the Orthodox the life of the Church has always flowed out from the presence of the Holy Spirit. Perhaps it would be better not to say that the Holy Spirit is 'at the heart of koinonia' but is indeed the 'heart' which gives life, Christ's life, to those reborn of water and the Holy Spirit. We find ourselves echoing Orthodox theology when it declares:

> The coming of the Holy Spirit in the Church is not an isolated historic event in the past, but a permanent gift which gives life to the Church, ensuring its existence in the history of humanity, making possible its witness to the inaugurated Kingdom of God. The Holy Spirit is the divine power whereby the Church is able to obey the command of the Risen Lord: 'Go forth then and make all nations my disciples' (Matt. 28:19) 'Go forth to every part of the world and proclaim the Good News to the whole creation' (Mark 16:15; cf. Luke 24:47-8 and Acts 1:8). This permanent Pentecostal outpouring of the Spirit on the Church is a reality in the Church's worship, in its public prayer, in the Sunday celebration of the Eucharist but it overflows the limits of ecclesial worship and constitutes the inner dynamic which gives character to all expressions of, and all activities in, the life of the Church'. (*Orthodox Thought*, Reports of Orthodox consultations organised by WCC 1975-82, ed. Genges Tsetes, WCC, Geneva, 1983, pp. 38-9)

The coming of the Spirit at Pentecost has often been seen as recovering the unity of the human family and reversing the disunity of Babel. The Spirit is the Spirit of unity. His permanent outpouring urges us constantly to rediscover our unity in Christ. I shall say more about the implications of koinonia for ecumenism later but at this point I want to indicate the inner unity and coherence which is characteristic of the new creation in Christ. As we explore the meaning of koinonia we are led to a better understanding of collegiality and co-responsibility within the Church, concepts and attitudes that have been recaptured and developed recently with the better understanding of the mystery of the Church. They merit our attention.

The Extraordinary Synod of 1985 reflected in depth on both concepts. Its final report stated: 'The ecclesiology of communion provides a sacramental foundation for collegiality.' The Catholic Church understands by collegiality that bishops are ordained to be members of a college which inherits the role and function of the apostles. This college with Peter as its head ensures the living communion of the churches. The College of Bishops can act collegially either in the strict sense or in a looser sense when the actions of some of its members are carried out in a collegial spirit even if the whole college is not involved.

We can therefore speak of collegiality which 'in the strict sense implies the activity of the whole College, together with its head, directed at the whole Church; its obvious expression is in an Ecumenical Council'.

But further, there are 'various partial realisations which are truly the sign and instrument of collegial spirit' (for example, Synod of Bishops, bishops' conferences, Roman Curia and so on).

The development of the collegial spirit has in recent years been one of the most vivid signs of new-found vitality within the Catholic Church. By it local churches are becoming increasingly aware of their unity and communion and are more readily and actively assuming responsibility for each other. Communion is now experienced as something horizontal as well as vertical. It is a one-ness with other local churches throughout the world as well as a unity in virtue of the relationship of each with Peter in Rome.

The other development making for greater unity and manifesting the permanent pentecostal outpouring of the Holy Spirit has been the growth of a sense of co-responsibility in each local church. The Extraordinary Synod's Final Report stated: 'Since the Second Vatican Council, a new type of collaboration between laypeople and clergy has happily come about in the Church . . . In this there is a new experience of the fact that we are all the Church.'

The preparatory working paper of the 1987 Synod declared: 'The sacraments of baptism and confirmation make the laity participants in the 'threefold office' of Christ, priestly, prophetic and kingly, entitling them to live the mission proper to the people of God' (N.23). We are coming to realise in practice as well as in theological theory that all the laity take an active, indispensable part in the action by which the risen Lord draws all things to himself in order to subject them ultimately, along with himself, to the Father 'so that God might be all in all'. They have a special place in the world and so, precisely as laity, they are called to accept the value of creation and, supported by grace, to relate it to God through their various activities, through their daily lives and work so that the kingdom of justice, love and peace might be established. All of Christ's faithful, all baptised members of the Church, are called first and foremost to share one communio, one koinonia. We are all to seek and find union with God and each other. We are to share one life of grace, one faith, one Eucharist, one mission; and all this before we are allotted particular ministries of service through ordination or forms of consecration.

So the ministries, the forms of life and service within the Church, are but different functions within the one mission and ministers are enriched with different charisms to serve the unity of Christ's body and to fulfil that single mission. The ideal of collaborative ministries, or, perhaps better, of interdependent ministries, provides us with a model of the Church and a living reality which more truly expresses the inner mystery of the Church. It is from this spirit that parish, deanery and diocesan councils are emerging, that the national committees and commissions are being formed to assist bishops' conferences and that forms of consultation and collaboration are being worked out at every level of the

Church. Thus a deepening awareness of koinonia is gradually reshaping the structures and life of the Church. Older concepts, more closely tied to models of authority and structure shared with secular society, are now giving way to a more conscious realisation in practice of the unique mystery and reality of the Church.

There can be little doubt that the rediscovery of the richness of koinonia is also gradually transforming our understanding of Christian ecumenism. It helps to explain both our fundamental unity which disunity has never succeeded in destroying and to provide us with the dynamic thrust towards full organic unity.

ARCIC, as already remarked, has been in the forefront of the exploration of koinonia and of its application to ecumenism. In the introduction to its final report the commission makes a crucial and fundamental statement: 'Although our unity has been impaired through separation it has not been destroyed. Many bonds still unite us. We confess the same faith in the one true God; we have received the same spirit; we have been baptised with the same baptism, and we preach the same Christ' (N.1).

The mutual recognition of the validity of Christian baptism has profoundly changed the relationships between separated Christians. The change has occurred within the last forty years. You have only to contrast the teachings of the Second Vatican Council with the approach taken even by Pius XII in the encyclical Mystici Corporis. In its time that document was truly prophetic and seminal. It is encouraging to note how far the Spirit has taken us in the past forty years:

> Despite the disagreements, men whose faith has brought them acceptance with God *in baptism* are incorporated in Christ. It is right that they should be distinguished with the name of Christian and they deserve to be recognised by the children of the Catholic Church as their brothers in the Lord. (UR. 3).

While, in Mystici Corporis, Pope Pius XII seemed to exclude others from fellowship: 'This true Church of Christ which is the Holy, Catholic, Apostolic, Roman Church . . .' (N.13) or again:

> As in the true community of the faithful there is but one Body, one Spirit, one Lord and one Baptism so there can be only one faith; and therefore whoever refused to hear the Church must, as the Lord commands, be considered as the heathen and the publican. It follows that those who are divided from one another in faith and government cannot be living in the one body so described and by the one divine Spirit. (Mystici Corporis, N.21)

The apparent contrast is stark. The implications of the former position taken up by Pius XII which was characteristic of the attitude of Roman Catholics until recently would seem to leave no alternative but to work for individual conversions and to await the withering away of other churches. After all, in that particular ecclesiology, those churches could offer no certain hope of salvation. Again it is encouraging to study the attitude of Mystici Corporis to other Churches with the present understanding expressed at the Council. It shows us how effectively and positively the Church has taken hold of the ecclesiology of Mystici Corporis and developed it.

Pope Pius XII also wrote: 'We invite them all (that is, those who do not belong to the visible structure of the Church) to yield their free consent to the inner stirrings of God's grace and strive to extricate themselves from a state in which they cannot be secure of their own eternal salvation' (Mystici Corporis, N.102).

None the less I think it is important to note that Pius XII was able to write concerning those who were not members of the visible Catholic Church: 'Though they may be related to the Mystical Body of the Redeemer by some unconscious yearning and desire . . .' with the clear hint that they are 'related' in some manner to the body of Christ. This very important statement was developed and broadened through the teaching of the Second Vatican Council and is expressed in Lumen Gentium.

The Fathers of the Council were explicit in their

acknowledgment that God worked outside the visible unity of the Roman Catholic Church:

> Many too of the sacred actions of the Christian religion are performed among our separated brethren. There is no doubt that they are capable of giving real birth to the life of grace in ways which differ according to the different nature of the individual Church or community and it must be granted that they are capable of giving admission to the community of salvation. (UR. 3)

It is now clearly understood – and this is a development not wholly grasped either inside or outside the Catholic community – that Catholics now recognise that when baptism is validly conferred at any time, inside or outside the visible unity of the Catholic Church, the person baptised is incorporated into Christ, is without doubt a member of Christ's body. Furthermore – and this again has far-reaching implications – the Catholic Church now recognises that 'a number of important elements or gifts from which the Church derives its structure and life, are capable of an existence beyond the confines of the visible Catholic Church'.

Inevitably Roman Catholics have to confront two sets of questions which are posed by this developing understanding. First, if every baptised person is incorporated into Christ what is the relationship between the visible institutional Church and the body of Christ? In what realistic sense can the Catholic Church claim to be the visible Church? Is there any need for an institutional Church at all? Secondly, if there are valid elements and gifts existing and operating outside the Catholic Church why should Catholics feel themselves under any urgent compulsion to tackle the immense institutional problems of Church unity? Why not let people remain where they are in the undisturbed enjoyment of the gifts of God? Why not accept separateness as evidence of diversity and not as disunity?

Certainly the answer to these questions must not be simplistic. To a greater extent than previously we have to recognise that it is foolish to attempt rigidly to institutionalise the life and love of God. He can never be confined to authorised channels. There must be a sincere and generous discernment of God's action in unexpected places, not only within Christian churches and assemblies but in other religious traditions altogether. It is a common failure among us all not to see the Spirit of God at work in the hearts of all humankind and in every aspect of human life and progress.

But, at the same time, we must be on guard against indifferentism. We have to make every effort to seek the certainty of absolute truth. Pius XII expressed the unwavering Catholic approach when he wrote in Mystici Corporis: 'It is an aberration from divine truth to represent the Church as something intangible and invisible, as a mere 'pneumatic' entity joining together by an invisible link a number of communities of Christians in spite of their differences in faith' (N.14).

The history of the people of Israel and of the Christian People of God surely points to the truth that God's action in the world takes on a definite shape, pattern and discernible purpose. In his dealings with mankind he takes account of our basic human need for community; he builds on nature. It is profoundly important, I believe, that the body of Christ, like its head, has to be both incarnate and sacramental. The Church, in the words of the Council is 'the sacramental or instrumental sign of intimate union with God and of unity for the whole human race' (Lumen Gentium, N.1). We need a visible Church, a welcoming, living community of faith and love. The world too needs the visible Church as witness to the indwelling of God in our race and as a sure sign of hope and reconciliation.

That brings us, I believe, to face the second set of questions. Does the visible Church need to be united? Is Christian unity an indispensable sign of God's action?

If the body of Christ, the Church, has to be visible because it has a mission in the world and for the world, must it also – to fulfil that mission be one? The message of the Gospel is, surely, weakened, its witness impaired if the voices which proclaim it are discordant and do not speak as one. There is, I am told, a Zulu proverb which says: 'I cannot hear what you say because of the thunder of what you are.'

Repeatedly we must return to our Lord's urgent prayer for

unity in the seventeenth chapter of St John's Gospel and
appreciate the priority that must be given to praying and
working for Christian unity. Koinonia inevitably underlines
the need for unity. We are baptised into the wholeness and
unity of God's life; the multiplicity and richness of his gifts
argue not for disunity and discord but for a veritable symphony and concord of minds and hearts in a single outpouring
of life and love. As Catholics we should be saying to our
separated brothers and sisters in Christ: 'We want you to
share all the riches that are part of the treasury of the Catholic
Church but we do at the same time recognise in each of you
aspects of your life in Christ which help to sustain and
encourage us in our discipleship of Christ.'

We are entering a new stage of our pilgrimage of faith. It is
far more than a matter of ecumenical good manners and
mutual tolerance. We are moving – in ways that have yet to be
agreed in practice – from ecumenical cooperation to a commitment in a joint search for our ultimate communion. We
must know each other better and not in order to refute and
correct but to appreciate and affirm. Indeed I am required by
the Catholic Church itself to respect and honour the riches
found in other churches. 'It is essential', declares the Council:

> that Catholics be pleased to recognise and set a value on
> the true Christian possessions which are found among the
> brethren separated from us and which derive from the
> common heritage. It is right and salutary to recognise
> the riches of Christ and the virtues at work in the life of
> others who bear witness to Christ, at times to the extent of
> shedding their blood. God is always marvellous and to be
> marvelled at in his work. (UR. 4)

I would, however, fail in my duty to unity and to truth if I did
not draw attention also to that aspect of Catholic teaching
which is uncompromising and uncomfortable. Recognition of
God's gifts in other churches in no way diminishes or denies
the Catholic Church's claim to uniqueness. The Council
document on ecumenism is at pains to state: 'The Catholic
Church possesses the wealth of the whole of God's revealed
truth and all the means of grace' (UR. 3). It is unable to
concede a similar status to others:

Our separated brethren do not have the benefit as individuals or in their communities and churches, of the unity which Jesus Christ has wanted to bestow on all those to whom he has given rebirth into a single body and into the new life, with the gift of a life in common; this is the unity proclaimed by the Sacred Scriptures and by the venerable tradition of the Church. (ibid.)

The Catholic Church cannot subscribe to a concept of the Church as a unity shattered into pieces by schism and heresy and now awaiting the coming together of the individual churches to remake the great Church of the future. That, I suspect, is a concept cherished by many outside the Roman Catholic Church but it cannot be embraced by us without fundamental violence to our understanding of Church and our reading of Christian history. We can do no other than affirm again in humility and faithfulness our conviction, restated at the Vatican Council: 'Only through the Catholic Church of Christ, the universal aid to salvation, can the means of salvation be reached in all their fulness. It is our belief that Christ entrusted all the benefits of the New Covenant to the Apostolic College over which Peter presides' (ibid.)

Then there is the crucial text in the Council's Constitution on the Church (N.8) which states that the Church of Christ 'subsists' in the Catholic Church 'under the government of Peter's successor'. That Latin word 'subsists' has to be translated by 'continues in' or 'to be found in'. The word 'subsist' was chosen in order not to deny that important elements of Christ's Church and sanctifying actions are to be found in other churches. I give the Latin text:

> haec ecclesia, in hoc mundo ut societas constituta et ordinata, *subsistit* in ecclesia Catholica, a successore Petri et Episcopis in eius communione gubernata, licet extra eius compaginem elementa plura sanctificationis et veritatis inveniantur, quae ut dona Ecclesiae Christi propria, ad unitatem Catholicam impellunt.

The reality of koinonia demands that our initial incorporation into the body of Christ and our imperfect but ever-growing share in the life and love of the Trinity should in God's good time issue forth into a communion and fellowship that is organic, sacramental and complete. In that flowering of koinonia we would all have to undergo not only profound structural changes but a radical metanoia, a change of heart, that might seem like a death but would be in fact a resurrection.

We are as yet in the earliest stages of that development. The concept of koinonia, held in sacred trust throughout history, now offers the promise of a bright future. Kaspar summed it up admirably when he wrote: 'The understanding of the unity of the Church as the unity of communio was the key to the ecumenical opening.' Armed with that key all of us can now explore the many mansions which house God's treasures of life and love.

I am however convinced that the concept of koinonia remains strangely incomplete if it is considered solely as having to do only with the inner life of the Church. God so loved the world that he gave his only-begotten Son to enter our world, take to himself our history, live, die and rise again for our sake and that of the whole human race. Christ made incarnate God's passion for justice and for the peace that springs from inner reconciliation. He came to bring good news to the poor, liberty to captives, new sight to the blind, freedom to the oppressed and God's year of favour to the whole people (Luke 4:18,19).

It is a work of healing and renewal, the working out in human relationships and society of the life and love God shares with his creation. All of this constituted the mission of Jesus Christ in his lifetime; it remains the mission of his body now and always. The Church as communion/koinonia has not a purely spiritual, other-worldly dimension but is the new and ongoing creation, the new heaven and new earth which are not merely to be longed for in the next life but are to be established here and now as the kingdom of heaven whose daily coming we pray for in the prayer we learned from the lips of Christ himself. Pope Paul VI loved to speak of the 'civilisation of love' the Church struggles to establish here and now. It is the building of the kingdom in the city of man, to which we have already committed ourselves and which we bring to birth daily in our lives and through all our actions.

3
Prophet, Priest, King

I suppose it would be true to say that the Catholic Church has never been more conscious than it is today of its unity and diversity. The Second Vatican Council, the assemblies of the International Synod of Bishops, the development of continental, regional and national bishops' conferences, the untiring pastoral journeys of Pope John Paul II which crisscross the globe, all the means of modern travel and communication, are shaping our awareness of unity but, at the same time, present us with a panorama of cultures, histories and present attitudes that remain gloriously different. In this the Church, the body of Christ and people of God, looks remarkably like the human race it sets out to reconcile and restore.

There is no more urgent and demanding task in Christian theology today than to explore and expound the nature of the Church as the mystery of God's communion with redeemed humanity. Intimately bound up with that study must be further reflection on baptism.

Before developing the idea of the Church as the people of God, it would be helpful to preface that consideration by dwelling a little on the Pauline image of the Church as the body of Christ. It tells us a great deal about the significance of baptism and sheds light on that unity and diversity which is characteristic of the Church as communio or koinonia.

The first letter of St Paul to the Corinthians contains a

chapter so beautiful that it usually stands alone. The hymn to charity or Christian love is so rightly celebrated that most overlook completely its context and full force. Chapters 10–14 make it quite clear that love is not an individual virtue or endowment but the flowering of an attitude which characterises the whole body of Christ. We love, just as we have faith and live in Christian hope, because we are baptised, are made members of the one body of Christ. Paul tells us, 'because there is one bread, we who are many are one body, for we all partake of the one bread' (1 Cor. 10:17); 'as often as you eat this bread and drink the cup, you proclaim the Lord's death until he comes' (11:26). In that one body, nourished and made one by the Eucharist, 'there are varieties of gifts, but the same Spirit; and there are varieties of service, but the same Lord; and there are varieties of working, but it is the same God who inspires them all in every one' (12:4–6). The outpouring of divine gifts whether it be the utterance of wisdom and knowledge, the gift of faith or healing or miracles, or prophecy or discernment or tongues, is evidence of that perpetual Pentecost whereby the Spirit enlivens the body of Christ. We are all members of that body in which we are incorporated by baptism. St Paul insists: 'just as the body is one and has many members, and all the members of the body, though many, are one body, so it is with Christ. For by one Spirit we were all baptised into one body – Jews or Greeks, slaves or free – and all were made to drink of one Spirit' (12:12–13). Every ministry in the Church needs the others; all are interdependent: 'The eye cannot say to the hand, I have no need of you', Paul reminds us forcefully. 'If one member suffers, all suffer together; if one member is honoured, all rejoice together' (12:21,26). The highest gift is that of love but we are to seek the spiritual gifts provided those are coordinated into a service worthy of God who 'is not a God of confusion but of peace' (14:33). It is a vision of the Church and of our Christian vocation which is sacramental and pentecostal and which expresses that unity in diversity which is both characteristic and unique.

It is important, I believe, to begin with the image of the Church as body of Christ if only to remind ourselves that no one image or model can ever adequately and exclusively express the whole truth about the Church and the mystery of our communion in the life and love of God. If I later lay stress on that image of the Church as people of God favoured to an extent by the Second Vatican Council in Lumen Gentium, I want to place alongside it both the image of the body of Christ as well as that concept of the Church which is now so central to all ecclesiological thinking: the idea of koinonia or communio which takes us deep into the inmost mystery of the Church.

Writing in his first letter to the churches of the Diaspora, the apostle Peter wrote:

> Christ is the living stone, rejected by men but chosen by God and precious to him; set yourselves close to him so that you too, the holy priesthood that offers the spiritual sacrifices which Jesus Christ has made acceptable to God, may be living stones making a spiritual house . . . you are a chosen race, a royal priesthood, a consecrated nation, a people set apart to sing the praises of God who called you out of the darkness into his wonderful light. Once you were not a people at all and now you are the people of God. (1 Peter 2:4–5,9–10)

Reflection on the theme of the Church as the people of God was the starting point chosen by Vatican II in the dogmatic Constitution, Lumen Gentium. That document reflected on the mystery of the Church using the images given in the scriptures: the sheepfold, the tract of land to be cultivated, the field of God, the true vine, the edifice of God, the spouse of Christ, the body of Christ (LG. 6–8). Such images are necessary for they give us the richness of symbolism necessary to explore that 'mystery', that life-giving sharing in God's life and love which is the Church. Yet of all these images the Fathers of the Second Vatican Council gave clear preference to one: the Church as the people of God. They devoted the whole of the second chapter of Lumen Gentium to the development of this image. They took it as their guide in describing both relationships within the Church and the goal or mission of the Church in the world (LG. 9–18).

In choosing the image of people of God, the Council Fathers deliberately emphasised certain themes. This way of speaking about the Church brings to the fore the continuity which links the Church with the people of Israel in God's plan of salvation for the whole of creation. This emphasis reminds us that the Church is an instrument and not an end in itself. The Church is the sacrament of salvation, 'its goal is the kingdom of God, which has been begun by God himself on earth and which is to be further extended until it is brought to perfection by him at the end of time' (LG. 9).

Secondly, the image of people of God lays stress on the human characteristics of the Church. We, the people of God, are Church because we respond to God's call, his invitation. And we respond with what we are and with what we have. We bring our humanity to this task, with its creativity and ingenuity, its strengths and weaknesses, its goodness and its waywardness. We are not perfect as we come to him who alone is able to make us fruitful.

Furthermore this image of the Church as people of God is helpful because it does not permit us to escape from the context of history. As a people we are firmly rooted in time and place and buffeted by all the winds of change which blow through human affairs. The fact that we bring our mind, hearts and wills to the service of God and open ourselves to his grace does not release us from that experience. Certainly we trust in his help and guidance, but we still face the dilemmas of change, movement and evolution. It is not surprising then, that the Council insisted that the Church is 'semper reformanda', always in need of forgiveness and renewal.

Finally this image of people of God was chosen, I am sure, because it helps to bring to the fore that which is common and fundamental to all Christians, namely the bond of baptism by which we are drawn into the fellowship of the people. This truth takes us beneath the distinctions of hierarchy and diversity of roles to a fundamental equality which is the source of that mutual respect and love which ought to characterise relationships within the people of God. Here is the antidote to elitism and clericalism: we are but one people, sharing one faith, one baptism, one Lord (cf. 'The Laity within the Ecclesial Community', *Pro Mundi Vita*, Bulletin 1056, 1986/3).

For all of these reasons the image of the Church as the people of God is particularly powerful as a foundation for reaffirming the role of the laity in the life and mission of the Church. Certainly neither this image nor the word 'laos' itself refers to one section of the Church exclusively. Both refer to the whole membership, the whole body; and both, as it were, 'predate' any distinction between clergy and lay. But precisely for this reason, the image gives us the correct context in which to explore the part to be played by the laity. 'People of God' reminds us of where we all stand together: as a sign to the world; as those who respond to God's call, subject to human history and in need of forgiveness, drawn together, made one, through our common baptism.

This perspective of Vatican II was strongly reaffirmed at the Extraordinary Synod of Bishops held in December 1985 on the twentieth anniversary of the ending of the Council. Some commentators have tried to make much of the fact that the actual phrase 'people of God' did not figure as strongly in the Final Report of the Extraordinary Synod as in the second chapter of Lumen Gentium. Personally I do not believe that is of any great consequence. The Final Report is a brief document, for the Extraordinary Synod itself was a brief meeting. Yet its main lines echo very closely, and give unequivocal affirmation to, the teachings of Vatican II. In the Final Report we are given a picture of the Church as that mystery by which we share in the life of God (koinonia), in which we are formed and nurtured by the scriptures and liturgical worship, so as to be the effective sacrament of salvation in our society. This directly reflects the main dogmatic and pastoral achievements of the Council: the Church as 'mystery' (Lumen Gentium), needing renewal through scripture (Dei Verbum) and liturgy (Sacrosanctum Concilium) in order to fulfil mission (Gaudium et Spes).

Reflection on the years before the Council underlines the importance of this emphasis in the development of the Church as people of God and, in particular, for the role of the laity. The 'Pro Mundi Vita' Dossier on the Laity, looking back to those pre-conciliar years, pinpoints four key ways in which the laity then were effectively excluded from crucial aspects of Church life, or communio. The lay person was largely excluded from the theology of the Church, for any understanding of the common priesthood and of the 'sensus fidelium' in the process of teaching had been largely forgotten. The lay person was given a purely passive role in ecclesiology at that time. Secondly, the laity were more or less effectively excluded from the patterns of spirituality, for married life and secular life were considered to be 'second class' and canonisations in practice were more or less reserved for priests, religious and martyrs. Thirdly, the laity were to a large measure excluded from active participation in the liturgy. And last, but by no means least, they were not in practice encouraged positively enough to read, reflect and pray the Bible. The changes brought about by Vatican II and solidly reaffirmed by the Extraordinary Synod can be seen very clearly in contrast to that brief and obviously inadequate sketch.

But let us return to the apostle Peter. In setting forth the image of the Church as the people of God he gives one necessary command. It is as if the validity of the image depends on this command. If it is not fulfilled then the truth at the heart of the image will be lost and an empty shell remain, capable of distortion and manipulation. Peter's command is simple. He says: if you are to be the people of God then you must 'set yourself close to Christ' (1 Pet. 2:5). In Christ alone there is source of life and, as Lumen Gentium, N.9 says, 'God has gathered together as one all who in faith look upon Jesus as the author of salvation and the source of unity and peace and has established them as the Church, that for each and all, she may be the visible sacrament of this saving unity' (LG. 9).

In other words, the people of God makes sense only when it is centred on Christ. Drawn by baptism into a communion of life with the Trinity and so called to share in the creative and redemptive task of the Word, the people of God draw their whole raison d'être, origin and purpose, from Christ himself. It is this fact that distinguishes the people of God and makes it utterly different from any democratisation of the Church constructed along the lines of western political models. It is this fact which establishes the radical difference between the people of God as the Church and national, continental or class groupings or identities, none of which can claim Christ exclusively for itself.

More positively, it is this fact which also helps us to explore more fully the characteristics of this people of God and to look closely at their richness, particularly as applied to the laity. For the characteristics of this people are a share, however imperfect, in the characteristics of Christ. He is, of course, divine and the sole mediator and we still struggle against our sinfulness, but we are united to him and as Church share his life and mission. Traditionally we speak of these characteristics of Christ as those of prophet, priest and king.

It is perhaps not surprising that these characteristics of Christ are spoken of as 'service to the community', and have been associated, in a particular way in the past, with the ordained ministry. According to Ignatius of Antioch it is bishops, with their helpers the priests and deacons, who have taken up this service of the community (Ad Philad, cf LG. 20), for it is they who are 'teachers of doctrine, priests of sacred worship and officers of good order' (cf. Clement of Rome, Ad Corinth.', cf. LG. 20). Yet, gradually, understanding of this 'service' has deepened, and Vatican II was able to assert that it is by virtue of baptism that participation in this threefold ministry of Christ is primarily established. Certainly there later came distinctions in role and responsibilities which are consequent upon ordination, but it is baptism which provides the right and duty of participation in these common tasks. I trust that it is not necessary to emphasise here that the Church is indeed not a democracy; although all the baptised share in the teaching and priestly ministry of Christ, none the less the ordained minister shares in that ministry in a manner that is different in kind and not just in degree. But notice words from Lumen Gentium: 'The laity are by baptism made one body with Christ and are established among the people of God. They are in their own way made sharers in the priestly, prophetic and kingly functions of Christ.' This teaching was reaffirmed later in Vatican II in the document on the Lay Apostolate when it stated that the laity 'have their own role to play in the mission of the whole people of God in the Church and in the world' and that 'incorporated into Christ's Mystical Body through baptism and strengthened by the power of the

Holy Spirit through confirmation, they are assigned to the apostolate by the Lord himself' (Apostolicam Actuositatem, N.2,3).

Now this is crucially important teaching and, I suspect, is still a long way from being fully assimilated into the life of the Church. For so many, people and priests alike, the involvement of the laity directly in the life and mission of the Church is still largely seen as an optional extra. It is taken up only when circumstances demand it, or more simply when survival depends on it. I suspect the common motivation for many in the development of the role of the laity is a combination of factors such as a comparative shortage of priests, an ageing priesthood, an increase in administrative burdens, a more educated laity willing to help. Fundamentally the motive is that of 'helping Father', and that is still a long way from the teaching presented by the Council. In fact the Council went even further and firmly rejected the notion that lay involvement was an extra, to be brought into operation when the priests were no longer able to manage on their own. Rather the Council starkly affirmed that 'the member of Christ's body who fails to make his proper contribution to the development of the Church must be said to be useful neither to the Church nor to himself' (AA. N.2).

This attitude of the Council is closely linked with the renewal called for in liturgical life. The Council said:

> Mother Church earnestly desires that all the faithful be led to that full, conscious and active participation in liturgical celebrations which is demanded by the very nature of the liturgy. Such participation by Christian people as 'a chosen race, a royal priesthood, a holy nation, a purchased people' (1 Pet. 2:9) is their right and duty by reason of their baptism.
>
> In the restoration and promotion of the sacred liturgy, this full and active participation by all the people is the aim to be considered before all else; for it is the primary and indispensable source from which the faithful are to derive the true Christian spirit. (Sacrosanctum Concilium, N.14)

Full and active participation in the life and mission of Christ is nourished and expressed by full and active participation in the liturgy of the Church. This is the vision of the people of God, and especially of the laity, held up by the Council. Drawn by baptism into that koinonia of God's life and love which finds its source and highest expression in the Eucharist, all the faithful are called to live that gift in the circumstances of each day, both in the contribution they make to the building up of the body of Christ, and in the witness they give in the world. An ecclesiology based on 'koinonia' can help us to recover the intimate bonds between Church and Eucharist. It can remind us that Eucharist, and the act of receiving Holy Communion, is never simply a private devotion, a matter of communion between disciple and Master, but it is also an expression of ecclesial communion, of belonging to the visible body, and thus of sharing with all the faithful directly in the mission of Christ to the world. In other words, where the Church is, there the Eucharist is; equally, wherever the Eucharist is there the Church is. This means, of course, that the manner in which we celebrate the Mass should look as if it is the whole Church which celebrates, and not just the priest. It should also be obvious that we are preparing for mission and not finding in worship a refuge from the realities of life.

It is important to look more closely at the characteristics of the people of God as prophet, priest and king, particularly as these apply to the laity in both the life and mission of the Church. The mission of the Church is that of Christ. The Church is to be the sacrament of the presence in the world of that creative Word through whom everything has life. The sending or 'missio' of the Spirit is constantly taking place, thus making present the Word so that all creation may be brought to that unity and integrity for which it is destined. As St Paul reminds us: 'creation still retains the hope of being freed, like us, from its slavery to decadence, to enjoy the same freedom and glory as the children of God' (Rom. 8:20–21).

This struggle for freedom, this 'groaning in one great act of giving birth', is the true context in which we must think about Christ, the prophet, priest and king and our sharing in his mission.

The prophet role, as presented to us in the Old Testament in particular, is that of bringing the Word of God face to face with particular circumstances. Christ is the prophet since what he embodies in his whole person is actually the Word of God. His coming into the world means that the world sees in him the realisation of what it should be. The baptised share in this by bringing the light of the Word to bear on the concrete circumstances of daily life. It is helpful to remember that one of the most important effects of hearing the Word of God is that a person comes to an acknowledgment of dependence on God. The two-edged sword of the Word cuts through to the marrow of self-reliance and brings the hearer first of all to the obedience of faith.

There are so many ways in which people today are helped to recognise, accept and live out their dependence on God and their interdependence on each other. Some are obvious, others perhaps surprising. Teachers and counsellors, sympathetic neighbours and corner-shopkeepers, doctors, Samaritans and delivery men often spend much time and effort accompanying others through times of difficulty, and in so far as this results in some deeper appreciation of the fundamental truths of our human condition then it is a sharing in the prophetic role of Christ. Others bear this same witness in their actions rather than their words, particularly those who bear suffering and hardship, not just with dignity but with that gracefulness which comes from God alone. Poverty, sickness and deprivation of themselves are ugly. Yet, with the grace of God, they become the raw material of some of the most startling prophetic witness in the world today. As the 'Instrumentum Laboris' for the Synod on the Laity pointed out: Many 'write with patience – and not without sufferings and struggle – the testament to a hope of eternal glory' (N.25).

In this task of proclaiming the Word for the benefit both of the Church community and of the Church's witness in the world, the laity are given as a gift of the Holy Spirit a 'supernatural appreciation of the faith'. In other words, as they face this task of bearing responsibility for the presentation of the faith in their own lives the baptised receive from the Holy Spirit a direct gift of understanding or 'sensus fidei', which can be described as an almost instinctive 'feel' for what is true, which is a gift from God and not necessarily an ability to reason accurately about him in technical terms. Sometimes it is suggested that the faith of the laity depends totally on the way it is taught and presented by the clergy. This is not true. Anyone who knows even a little of the history of the Church in England and Wales, Scotland and Ireland, knows that for many decades of the Reformation period the well-being of the faith was in the hands of the laity. Families, of the rich and poor alike, risked life and wealth to protect and preserve the faith, to harbour the priest and to keep alive and active that deep love of the Mass which is so central to a living faith. Those who by virtue of their baptism share in the prophetic mission of Christ ought to be relied upon. Mistrust and suspicion should not be part of relationships within the Church. Rather an openness by all to the Word of God, and a willingness to engage in open debate as part of the search for truth, should characterise that body, the Church, whose task it is to bear witness to the presence of the Spirit of truth, poured out on all creation. A necessary consequence of this understanding is that pastors should feel it essential at all times to listen with the utmost attention and respect to the insights, experience and judgments of the laity who themselves are possessed of the Spirit.

Similarly all the baptised share in the task of Christ, the king of all creation. The kingdom proclaimed by Christ is characterised by 'justice, love, truth and peace' (cf. Preface of Christ the King). The daily task of edging creation nearer to this reality is a direct participation in the kingly office of Christ. There are many whose tasks include the establishment or maintenance of 'good order' (cf. LG. 20). These tasks may be undertaken on the street or in the classroom; in the workshop, research laboratory or management office; in the courts and civic authorities. Wherever such tasks are fulfilled in a way that searches for justice and is free from deliberate prejudice and corruption, then the kingly role of Christ is being lived out and baptismal responsibilities fulfilled.

Within the life of the Church, too, the same is true. There too there are offices of good order to be fulfilled, in which the search for justice must be paramount. The good ordering of the Church's own life, the exemplary manner in which all people are treated with justice and compassion, is an integral part of the Church's mission and not simply a 'domestic affair'. The scandal of injustice within the Church, and the occasional lack of good order, seriously weaken the effectiveness of our mission. All the baptised have a duty to contribute to the inner credibility of the Church not least by keeping in mind the statement of Lumen Gentium that the laity 'by reason of their knowledge, competence or outstanding ability, are permitted and sometimes even obliged to express their opinion on things which concern the good of the Church' (LG. 37). At the same time we must not forget that there is leadership in the Church. The Pope has a special authority, and so do the bishops. It is frequently forgotten in these days that there is, too, an obedience to be shown, and obedience is an important virtue. Without it the body loses coherence and direction. We often endure within the Church the confusion which results from the indiscriminate pursuit of private judgment.

The Council declared: 'With the help of the Holy Spirit, it is the task of the entire people of God, to hear, distinguish and interpret the many voices of our age and judge them in the light of the Divine Word' (The Role of the Church in the Modern World, N.44). The prophetic office of Christ finds its expression, therefore, in the whole body of Christ.

It is the mission of Christ to restore all things to the Father. He is the Word through whom all things were made and he is the reconciliation of all things into that final peace and unity which is God's kingdom. Our promise and foretaste of this is the liturgy of the Church, in which minds and hearts are raised to God and, in Christ, brought into that unity of life and love which only he can achieve. This is the priestly office of Christ, the raising up to God of all things as an offering of praise and worship.

We participate in this office of Christ, then, whenever we help to raise mind and heart to God in awe, worship and praise. Artists and poets, musicians and sculptors, are often among those who through their work cause people to pause and to ponder, to catch a glimpse of the majesty of creation or the pathos and dignity of human effort and so to raise mind and heart to the transcendent God. Human creativity and artistry must be seen as part of the priestly function of God's people. The faithful clearly fulfil their office also by the conscious offering of themselves and their daily tasks to the

Father. Through those efforts, daily life is made holy, the invisible but ever-present God is pointed to and others can recognise the witness of service and prayer.

Within the Church it is the responsibility of the priestly office to care for the quality and integrity of praise and worship. The ordained priest by virtue of ordination plays a key role in public worship, presiding over the community at Mass, consecrating the gifts of bread and wine, and ministering the sacraments. Catholic theology and devotion down the centuries have seen the ordained priest as acting 'in persona Christi', the very embodiment of Christ. Conscious of such dignity priests have striven to be worthy of it, despite human frailty. It is a tradition of great beauty and depth. It helps a priest to appreciate his specific vocation in the Church and to fulfil his role humbly yet joyously. He is called to take his place in the community as representing its Head as well as its members. He is bound, therefore, to carry out his liturgical function and fulfil his responsibility so that the people of God may properly appreciate what is signified and what is effected in each Eucharist, the eternal self-offering of Christ to the Father. Many others, naturally, share in this responsibility today, through preparation of the liturgy and through extending its celebration into the homes of those who cannot be present personally. Lectors, cantors, readers, extraordinary ministers of the Eucharist are but some of the ways in which lay people share actively today in the priestly office of Christ in the Church. These are to be welcomed for they help to achieve that 'full and active participation' called for by the Council.

Cardinal Cardijn, that great apostle of the modern laity, used to say: 'No work – no Mass.' In other words the offering to the 'God of all creation' must always embrace the lives and work of all the faithful. Their labour makes the sacrifice possible, contributes to all its elements, is enriched and blessed by the shared offering.

No deep separation should be established between the Church in its internal life and the Church in relation to the world. The very internal life of the Church is, after all, a noble and historical manifestation of the Church as sacrament. It is unsatisfactory to speak of the role of the laity as belonging solely to the secular world, the internal life of the Church being the domain of the clerics and their few assistants. The life of the Church is 'communio' and as such must consist of those relationships of shared life and love, shared gifts and responsibilities which themselves witness to the saving truth of the Gospel.

Nevertheless there is a constant need to remind ourselves that the Church does not exist for its own sake. Our task is not merely to establish and enjoy good participative relationships within the Church. These are but means; means by which all must be enabled to bear witness to Christ in society. Sometimes withdrawal into Church affairs and preoccupation with its parochial and diocesan life is, unfortunately, motivated by a one-sided perception that the world is a Godless place and that involvement in its affairs involves compromise and sometimes the abandonment of absolute standards and ideals.

Undoubtedly aspects of contemporary society are hostile to the Gospel, but the relationship of the Church to the world should not be that of attack and confrontation. For the world and all of creation is the work of God's hand and the dwelling-place of the Holy Spirit. Christians in the world are not invaders in a foreign territory but servants of the Lord attentive to the signs of his presence, waiting to catch the breeze of his Spirit wherever it may blow. It is for them under that influence to discern the beauty that may have become disfigured and to work to restore it through lives of love, reconciliation and justice.

'Set yourselves close to Christ' says St Peter. The Christ to whom we must be close, if we are to share in his tasks of prophet, priest and king, is the Christ of creation, the Pantocrator. It is he who is the perfect Man, bringing all creation to its fullness. The scene of our cooperation with Christ is as wide as the world itself. There is no place in which the baptised cannot fulfil their high calling, in which the Word of God cannot be proclaimed, the good order of his kingdom fashioned and the obedient worship of the Father offered. In the Church we do this, rejoicing in the gift of faith; but it is in society today that our gifts are needed and God's fruitfulness longed for so that God might be 'all in all'.

4

Ministry and Ministers

The Synod on the Vocation and Mission of the Laity in the Church and the World provided clear proof that the question of ministry is regarded everywhere as a matter of considerable pastoral and theological importance. The fact that it touches on the question of women and their equality and dignity in the life of the Church has increased public interest.

Ministry is not something we can explore or talk about in isolation. In fact it is precisely because it has often been considered in isolation that some of the present difficulties have arisen. We have to keep before our eyes a vision and theology of the whole Church so that what we say about ministry has the right context. A true picture of ministry can be formed only if there is a proper understanding of the Church.

One of the important aspects of the Second Vatican Council was its rediscovery and affirmation of a more profound and scriptural approach to the understanding of the Church. The original treatment proposed for the theme of the Church was predictably structural and juridical. This was quickly rejected. The essence of the approach eventually agreed is indicated in the title given to the first chapter of the eventual Constitution, 'The Mystery of the Church'. The Council taught that the Church is a sacrament: 'a sign and an instrument of communion with God and of unity among men' (LG. 1). Immediately we are being led into contemplation of the

inner life and love of the Trinity and are led to see the Church
on earth as sharing that life and love. Lumen Gentium says
that 'the Holy Spirit was sent on the day of Pentecost in order
that he might continually sanctify the Church and that, consequently, those who believe might have access through Christ
in one Spirit to the Father' (LG. 4).

The Second Vatican Council drew upon the rich store of
scriptural images to describe the Church. Taken either from
the life of the shepherd or from cultivation of the land, from
the art of building or from family life and marriage, these
images were first fashioned in the books of the prophets and
applied in the New Testament to the Church. The striking and
familiar image found first in St Paul's letters is that of the
Church as body of Christ. That community is nourished and
made one both by the Eucharist which is the body and blood
of Christ himself and by the Word of God which is the
self-revelation of God in the scriptures. Made one with Christ
through baptism we are called to be part of the same ministry
that Christ began in his own lifetime. He claimed in the
synagogue at Nazareth that he had come to fulfil the prophecy
of Isaiah:

> The spirit of the Lord is upon me,
> because he has anointed me to preach
>   good news to the poor.
> He has sent me to proclaim release
>   to the captives
> and recovering of sight to the blind,
> to set at liberty those who are
>   oppressed,
> to proclaim the acceptable year of
>   the Lord.
>
> (Luke 4:18–19)

His is a mission of reconciliation and redemption, of healing
and setting free. Christ accepted that mission from the
Father; it is now the mission of the Church since the Church is
his continuing sacramental presence in and for the world. His
mission and ministry are ours through baptism. No one
should diminish or deny our active and full sharing in that

single mission and the fundamental equality and dignity of all the baptised.

Just to describe the Church as one body, one people in communion, would be to lose sight of the dignity and freedom of the individual. The Council emphasised the role of the individual: 'There is a common dignity of members deriving from their rebirth in Christ . . . there is, then, no inequality arising from race or nationality, social condition or sex' (LG. 22). Each person has gifts and talents which are God-given, Spirit-inspired and which are a gift not only to the individual but to the community as a whole. Here, very clearly, the Church enjoys both diversity and unity. St Paul tells us that 'To each is given the manifestation of the Spirit for the common good' (1 Cor. 12:7). Then, as St Paul begins to specify these gifts, a picture begins to emerge of a community young in experience but rich in charisms:

> To one is given through the Spirit the utterance of wisdom, and to another the utterance of knowledge according to the same Spirit . . . to another the working of miracles, to another prophecy, to another the ability to distinguish between spirits, to another various kinds of tongues, to another the interpretation of tongues. (12:8,10)

This account of the early Church takes for granted that when the Spirit seizes a group of believers, new and surprising energies are released which can best be described as the pentecostal outpouring of God's Spirit. We are dealing here with the shared communion of God's life and love to which all the baptised are equally called.

Yet St Paul, in writing to the young Church at Corinth, does not hesitate to discern and to arrange. In Chapter 14 he lays down the general principle that all things are to be done for strengthening the Church. He specifies that 'if any speak in a tongue, let there be only two or at most three, and each in turn; and let one interpret' (1 Cor. 14:27). He makes further provision for prophecy and concludes 'God is not a God of confusion but of peace' (14:33). Diversity is to be brought back into unity. Here then we can begin to see how important it is to harness and guide developments in the life and work of the Church so that the single mission of Christ might more effectively be realised.

Certainly it took the first Christian communities very little time to realise that if Christ's mission were to be continued there had to be some organisation and visible structure so that each member of the community could have specific responsibility and office. In the Acts of the Apostles, Chapter 6, we read of almost immediate dissension and grumbling in the Church at Jerusalem. There were accusations of favouritism in the distribution of help to an ethnic group of widows. It led the Twelve to summon the disciples so that they might select 'seven men of good repute, full of the Spirit and of wisdom, whom we may appoint to this duty' (Acts 6:3). It is important to note that the initiative was taken by the pastors in response to expressed needs, that 'the disciples' chose the candidates and that the pastors ratified the choice, laid hands on the seven and they began to serve the community.

There is no need at this point to rehearse the whole teaching of the Dogmatic Constitution on the Church, Lumen Gentium. It clearly lays down how bishops inherit the tasks and the ministry originally entrusted to the college of apostles with Peter at its head. They themselves are represented in each local gathering of the faithful by priests who 'render the universal Church visible in their locality and contribute efficaciously towards building up the whole body of Christ' (LG. 28). All the baptised 'are placed in the people of God, and in their own way share the priestly, prophetic and kingly office of Christ and to the best of their ability carry on the mission of the whole Christian people in the Church and in the world' (LG. 31). This sharing in a single mission calls for a spirit of unity and mutual love. The sheer diversity of graces, ministries and works which gathers the children of God into a single body must be *subject* to those called by God to lead and guide the flock.

This then, is the context of ministry. Each expression of ministry must be recognised, affirmed and integrated into the mission of the Church by the pastor, the bishop of a diocese. It is part of his pastoral concern for that part of the people of God entrusted to his care. At the risk of tedium it is important to spell out the consequences because there is a good deal of confusion on this subject and some clarity in terminology and usage will be helpful. The confusion of ideas has arisen, I believe, for two major reasons.

In the first place, when speaking of ministries within the Church we become immediately aware of a certain poverty of language. The term 'ministry' almost becomes an umbrella under which a number of different concepts take shelter. Too many types of work and service have been simply, and I venture to suggest misleadingly, called 'ministry'.

In the second place, ministry has suffered from a diversity of approach. Rules and regulations have been introduced without reference to the overall picture of what ministry is within the Church. So we are again faced with a confusion of ideas.

The present position is this. First, there is the clearly defined ministry which is conferred by the sacrament of orders. The Constitution on the Church, Lumen Gentium, was very clear in its definition: 'the divinely instituted ecclesiastical ministry is exercised in different degrees by those who even from ancient times have been called bishops, priests and deacons' (LG. 28). They are ministers by ordination because they have been called by God to a very specific vocation of service. This group is clearly defined, since all are ministers by virtue of the sacrament. There are none – even enclosed monks of the strictest observance – who after receiving the sacrament of holy orders are not participating in ministry.

Secondly, there are also two lay ministries that have been specifically so described. They are the ministry of acolyte which is a eucharistic ministry and the ministry of lector which is a service concerned with the Word of God. These ministries, which had been in existence since the days of the early Church, were re-instituted by Pope Paul VI in his Motu Proprio 'Ministeria Quaedam' in 1973. In that document the minor orders conferred in the past as part of the preparation for priesthood were suppressed and were replaced by the ministries of lector and acolyte. By this new disposition the Pope wanted to underline the distinction between the clerical and the lay state. Now no one was to become a cleric before ordination to the diaconate, but these ministries could be conferred both on lay people and on candidates for priestly ordination. In fact much of the confusion and difficulty concerning the ministries of acolyte and lector arise from the fact that they are also required to be conferred on future priests prior to their ordination to the diaconate. It was made clear in that document that women were excluded from such ministries, a provision which has in point of fact persuaded some bishops' conferences not to adopt these ministries in their countries for lay people. It was also stated in the document that other ministries could be added by bishops' conferences as circumstances required. So far, however, this has not happened.

Thirdly, the notion of ministry is often used in a very broad sense as any service which is rendered by the baptised in union with Christ. The Second Vatican Council sometimes employed the term in this sense. In certain parts of the Church there appears to be the practice of regarding all service of others as in some sense 'ministry' and as sharing the ministry of Christ. So that all service, every Christian activity, is thought of as a ministry of the Church and the individual as a minister. I am not persuaded that this is helpful, or indeed right.

There is an obvious need here for some clarification and coherence. The new Code of Canon Law has clearly described the rights and obligations of the laity and the way they are called to share positively in the mission of the Church. The manner of expression is, as one would expect, sober and juridical. Canon 225 tells us:

> Since the laity like all the Christian faithful are deputed by God to the apostolate through their baptism and confirmation they are thereby bound by the general obligations and enjoy the general right to work as individuals or in associations so that the divine message of salvation becomes known and accepted by all persons throughout the world.

The canon goes on: 'This obligation has a greater impelling force in those circumstances in which people can hear the Gospel and know Christ only through lay persons.' Here we have explicit recognition that there are circumstances in which the mission of Christ can be fulfilled *only* through the laity. Another canon is even more explicit:

> When the necessity of the Church warrants it and when ministers are lacking, lay persons, even if they are not lectors or acolytes, can also supply for certain of their offices, namely, to exercise the ministry of the word, to preside over liturgical prayers, to confer baptism and to distribute Holy Communion in accord with the prescriptions of the law. (Canon 230.s3)

The Church then, recognises that the laity not only have a ministry common to all Christian faithful which is a sharing in the mission of the whole Church, but at times and in some circumstances must accept a good deal of responsibility for the exercise of this missionary activity. They can perform the functions of ministry even if not formally invested with an official ministry.

It is also clear that in the life of the Church there are other activities and service which are not recognised as ministries in the same sense that lector and acolyte are. They are however every bit as important for mission. They too call for specific recognition and careful training which sets people apart from other faithful who have a general obligation for the mission of the Church. One of these groups would obviously be catechists. Canon Law tells us:

> Local Ordinaries are to see to it that catechists are duly prepared to fulfil their task correctly, namely, that continuing formation is made available to them, that they acquire a proper knowledge of the Church's teaching and that they learn in theory and practice the norms proper to pedagogical disciplines. (Canon 780)

The specific contribution made by the catechist in old and new churches alike needs no further commendation; in mission territories particularly their role is irreplaceable. Yet the function of the catechist has not yet been accorded the same ecclesial recognition as those ministries specifically related to the sacred liturgy.

I have indicated the present situation only briefly. It is clear that it is unsatisfactory and confusing. There are things to criticise and things which require constructive reform. The present structure is unsatisfactory if we look in particular at those formal ministries of acolyte and lector. They were intended as lay ministries but in practice they also remain clerically directed. Those destined for the priesthoood are being commissioned temporarily for these ministries. They are exclusively male ministries even though a guiding principle in the revision of the Code was to alleviate wherever possible any discrimination between men and women. It is also unsatisfactory that no new ministries have been added in more than a decade although the possibility has always existed. There is further confusion about the commissioning of ministers and the extent of their commission and the manner of their installation.

In October 1987 at the Synod of Bishops in Rome I ventured to suggest a possible clarification of ministry. I thought it would be helpful to apply a single structure to the whole field of ministry, a structure securely rooted in our vision of the Church and ordered to an effective participation in the mission of the Church. I suggested that we restrict the term ministry and ministers to actions and people who in some way represent the community of believers officially and act with the authority of the bishop or his delegate. This is in no way to deny or diminish the universal call and responsibility of all members of Christ's body to be his presence in our world. This we all do when as the people of God we go about our daily work, encouraging, building up, giving witness, growing in personal holiness. But all that generalised, individual and constant activity is best described as Christian apostolate; all ministry is apostolate, not all apostolates are ministry. To that apostolate, under the inspiration of the Holy Spirit, we bring all our talents and gifts. But there is a more specific and restricted meaning of ministry and ministers.

I suggested at the synod that these can fall into three categories, the ordained, the instituted and the commissioned. Some would argue that it might be best to restrict the concept and name of ministry strictly to the ordained and instituted ministries, that is, to those which specifically build up the body of Christ in word and in sacrament, and so consider the commissioned ministries as rather the fulfilment of mission. But that must remain, for the present, entirely tentative and debatable.

The first group of ministers I spoke of at the synod is made up of those people who because of their particular expertise, talents and role are commissioned by the local church community for specific tasks over a particular, limited period. These – if we are to give them a name – would be 'commissioned' ministers. In this group would come, for example, those who administer the affairs of a parish or diocese, who exercise hospitality and extend a welcome on behalf of a community, who carry out the task of caring for the elderly and housebound in any area. An architect, artist or builder engaged by a parish to complete a church, school or community building could also be commissioned until the completion of the task. Members of parish councils, youth leaders, delegates to conferences, those who plan and lead in pastoral liturgy could also be set aside and commissioned to act in the name of the community. Such commissioned ministry would concern people who not only engage in the Christian apostolate and share the Church's mission in a general way but who in addition are also called to more specific service within the community or on behalf of the community because they have specific gifts or undertake specific responsibilities. Such a ministry could be described as an office and can be conferred with or without any particular form of liturgical celebration. The ministry would last as long as the particular work undertaken; the parish or pastoral council members, for example, would be commissioned for the period of their membership; the musician would remain commissioned for as long as he or she accepted that community service.

I can see merit in recognising this kind of service as ministry. It is right that individuals should be recognised and affirmed when they undertake work of significance for the community. Some of these tasks go far beyond the building up of the body of Christ and have more to do with mission. I could see this myself as an expression of the idea of the parish living and working 'in council', that is as a living organism. We are gradually accepting the idea of parish councils as a way of developing genuine co-responsibility and realising the ideal of communion in a local place. We would need to go beyond that, at least on occasions and for particular areas of concern, with the development of the idea that the parish, building on its sacramental unity, should formally and corporately act in fulfilment of Christ's mission in a particular place. Then the parish, under the leadership of its pastor, can approve candidates for this kind of ministry, commission them in the name of the community, receive reports from those now formally accountable to it and sustain and encourage them throughout their period of service. One example could be the sending of a young person to work in a Third World country. In this kind of way, without diminishing the involvement of each of the baptised, the parish or diocese could corporately further the mission which Christ claimed for himself in the synagogue of Nazareth. And ministry undertaken in this way in the name of the community can, experience shows, transform and renew the personal commitment and idealism of such a commissioned minister.

The second category of ministry and minister can be described as 'instituted'. Here we follow much more closely the idea of ministry expressed by Pope Paul VI in 'Ministeria Quaedam'. These ministries should be conferred on laity and concern the sacramental life of the Church. They differ from 'commissioned' ministries by requiring a long-term commitment on the part of the minister and are inaugurated by a ceremony of installation to bestow the office. Instituted ministers would be prepared for their role and sustained by preliminary and in-service training provided by the bishop within his diocese. Candidates would be those whom the bishop – or his advisers – thought suitable for the task. Ministry of this kind would also be public in character since it would be closely connected with the liturgy and with the communication of God's word. The two ministries of lector and acolyte named by Pope Paul VI in 'Ministeria Quaedam' fit well into the ministries of word and sacrament, but others could be added. I mentioned earlier the ministry of catechist.

While everyone in the Church plays a part in communicating the faith, and a special responsibility rests with parents and godparents, there is an obvious ministry for those who undertake this task in a more public and formal fashion. I would also suggest that, given the priority attached to pastoral care of the family in our day and the urgent need to promote stable and happy family life, that of marriage counsellor might well be included in these 'instituted' ministries. The link with the sacrament of marriage is close and obvious. Much pioneering ministry is being carried out in these days by parish sisters and pastoral assistants. They are enriching the whole practice of pastoral care. Their service would seem to me to constitute an instituted ministry. As far as other forms of service are concerned, even those closely associated with the sacraments, I would argue for restraint in the creation of such ministries. These latter must meet obvious and pressing needs of the community; they must have a clear link with the sacramental life of the Church and the proclamation of the Word of God and care must be taken lest their proliferation lead to an unwelcome and unnecessary clericalising of the laity. These ministries need not be of universal institution. In fact it is expected that they will be created by the conference of bishops in response to national and diocesan needs and circumstances. They should be open to both men and women. They should be truly lay and not regarded as steps to the priesthood. Baptism is reason for ministry, a share in Christ's role of prophet, priest, king. The 1987 Synod of Bishops gave consideration to these matters and to 'Ministeria Quaedam'. The Fathers were in favour of reviewing that document in the light of local experience and needs. Here too, I would suggest, we might well have things to learn by listening carefully to other Christian churches and evaluating their extensive experience.

Since 'instituted' ministry is different and separate from 'commissioned' ministry, so both are different and separate from the third category, the sacred or ordained ministry. Ordained ministers are called by God to a lifelong commitment for which they are carefully prepared, and that calling and preparation are sealed by a sacramental character in ordination. It is a service of others in collaboration with the bishop or with their superiors even if they are ordained in Institutes of Consecrated Life. The three orders within this sacred ministry – bishops, priests, deacons – have been attested as early as the second century and were confirmed by the Second Vatican Council. Inevitably at a time of profound social change and theological development the role and ministry of the ordained is subject to many pressures and is undergoing something of a transformation. The theological perception of the Church as koinonia or communio and the diminishing emphasis on structural hierarchy has very profound consequences for the way we perceive ordained ministry. The bishop and the priest who represents him at parish level is no longer seen at the lonely but all-powerful pinnacle of a pyramid but is the heart of a community, exercising a ministry of word and sacrament, the symbol and source of that unity and communion of faith and love which is the local church. The way the ordained ministry is carried out reflects a developing theology of Church. No longer is it appropriate for the priestly ministry to be exercised in splendid isolation and with a semblance of sanctified autocracy. The sharing of the whole people of God in Christ's mission and ministry calls for consultation, collaboration and sharing.

Having said that, however, I would not wish to belittle in any way the authority which belongs to the priest in virtue of his sharing in the ministry of the bishops in the particular church, which is the diocese. Parish priests do, and must, make decisions. Not everyone finds this easy. Many tensions can build up in a parish or a diocese if pastors or people ignore the unique bond which binds them into a single body in Christ. We are not to think in terms of superiority and power but of loving service, each recognising in the other the face and the presence of Christ. For the community to grow in the life and love of God the ministry of the bishops as service and centre of unity in the name of Christ has to be acknowledged and respected. The priest who shares the ministry of the bishop in respect of his particular parish should accept his responsibility and be accepted by his parishioners in the same spirit. His authority is not conferred by members of the community but exists in virtue of his ordination and for the sake of the community. A deeper understanding of the mystery of the Church is bound to affect both the exercise and the acceptance of authority within the Church.

In response to the National Pastoral Congress in 1980 our bishops of England and Wales wrote:

It is our belief that the more effective the truly Gospel-inspired role of the lay person, the more satisfying the spiritual role and the clearer the ministerial identity of the priest. True collaboration does not blur distinction between ministries. It clarifies the distinction and shows the ministries to be complementary in the life and mission of the family of the Church. (Easter People, 30).

The new understanding of the Church is slowly but surely transforming our attitudes and our practice. With the re-emergence of a more scriptural understanding all our patterns of pastoral relationships are undergoing a radical reappraisal. One of the consequences of a theology of koinonia and of our growing awareness that all the baptised share intimately the life and love of the Triune God is that we learn a deeper sense of trust in God and in each other. Trusting each other, we have to listen to each other as possessing in some measure the Spirit of God. We each have something valuable to contribute to the other, each has a unique witness to give. Since Christ has entrusted his Church to all of us, we are in turn called to deepen our own trust in his Spirit and in each other. This must lead us to a Church which listens, which learns, which is prepared to work in a spirit of collaboration without manipulation and discrimination.

In the 1987 Synod part of this process was described as 'collaborative ministry'. A lay observer from England, Miss Pat Jones, was the first to outline this concept to the bishops. She described it as 'laypeople, priests and religious sharing their gifts, working together in mutual trust and commitment'. She went on:

We need collaboration in ministry because it reveals the nature of the Church most effectively. We need it because it is in itself a communal formation for the whole parish.

When people see ministry that is collaborative they understand what it means to say 'we'. They gain confidence and
motivation for their own involvement in ministry and
mission . . . Most importantly, collaborative ministry
means that formation can be available for all rather than a
few because it draws more people into leadership. It calls
for the recognition and employment of the endless gifts of
God to the people as a priority in pastoral planning.

The concept and its realisation in practice offer, I believe, the
best way forward in developing parishes and communities
which are capable of transforming their local situation. Collaborative ministry is an example of that interdependence
which should be characteristic of the Church and of all our
human experience. Collaboration and sharing are not easy to
achieve or maintain. They cannot survive if they are seen as
little more than power-sharing. The Church is not an institution dedicated to the pursuit and exercise of power. Ministry
by its very definition is concerned with service. Collaborative
ministry then is the fruit of that metanoia which involves
death to assertiveness and a letting go of self-interest. It can
flourish only when ministers are prepared to be channels of
God's love and healing for others and to recognise the image
and life of God in others.

Collaboration and interdependence are essential if we are
ever to transcend practices, habits of thought and ways of
exercising ministry which owe more to dualism than to
communio or koinonia. Many create a dichotomy between
the sacred and the secular, and that can lead to an unrealistic
response in the Church. It is wrong, however, to assume that
the inner life of the Church and the parish is best left to the
ordained clergy while the redemption of secular society is
exclusively the preserve of the laity.

We are coming slowly to understand that any such dualism
cannot be sustained. The one body of Christ has a single
mission and ministry, differently realised, to one world, one
humanity, one creation. To this ministry and mission all the
baptised are called although some are called subsequently to a
further ordained ministry. In every sphere, whether regarded
as sacred or secular, the whole people of God is involved.

One consequence is that ordained and lay ministers have a collaborative role in both the Church and the world; lay ministers have much to contribute to the sacred and the ordained to the secular.

There is not as yet a clear and universal appreciation throughout the people of God of the splendour of their vocation and mission. Too often there remains that implied dualism, a gulf between faith and life, between what is involved in membership of the Church and the rest of secular life and its responsibilities. We have to beware of making distinctions into divisions. The Second Vatican Council took pains to avoid this and maintains a unity which we have not always managed to achieve in practice. Its Decree on the Laity stated:

> The lay people, as they set about accomplishing this mission of the Church, work as apostles both in the Church and out in the world, among spiritual realities and among the things of our world For even if there is a difference between these two, the spiritual and the transient, in the one and only plan of God they are so bound together that it is the whole universe he intends to bring back to himself creating it afresh in Christ. (AA. 5)

As a final reflection on this new creation in Christ, we cannot leave to one side an issue which emerged in the 1987 Synod of Bishops as of major concern in many parts of the world. I refer of course to the place of women in the Church and the world. It is relatively easy – and entirely human – for us to argue for equality of dignity and opportunity for women in the world while denying in practice that same equality of women in the Church. I have already indicated when speaking of instituted and commissioned ministries that I take it as entirely reasonable that they should be open equally to women. The admission of women to the ordained ministry is another matter altogether and it is a question that has created new problems for the movement towards Christian unity. Throughout the present controversy within the Church of England I have consistently argued that this is a step of such gravity and one which is at such variance with the constant practice of the

Catholic and Orthodox churches throughout the whole of Christian history that it should not be taken without the prior agreement of the whole Church. Popes in recent years have argued with great forcefulness that this is not an open question and that there are no grounds in scripture, theology or tradition for admitting women to this form of ministerial service. That said, however, there is every reason to reappraise our present dispositions and practices towards women in the Church and to ensure that none is conditioned by past social and cultural discrimination. The guiding text might be the letter of St Paul to the Galatians: 'For as many of you as were baptised into Christ have put on Christ. There is neither Jew nor Greek, there is neither slave nor free, there is neither male nor female; for you are all one in Christ Jesus' (3:27–28). The believer is liberated from blind nationalism without ceasing to be a patriot; from the constraints of social status without ceasing to respect civil authority and from all forms of sexual discrimination without ceasing to recognise the complementarity and distinction of men and women.

No one can deny that the emancipation of women has been a slow and hotly-contested process in human history up to, and including, the present day. It has to be recognised as one of the genuine signs of the times. The Church must not be dragged reluctantly in the wake of progress but should be in the vanguard of those who recognise and struggle to achieve equality and equal dignity for women. It has been a worrying trend of recent years that at least in some parts of the world women seem to have become disillusioned with what they regard as the Church's reluctance to accord them their true role and in some numbers have ceased to play an active part in the life and work of the Church. We have for so long taken for granted the devotion and faithfulness of women in the Church that we may fail to see the warning signs until it is too late.

There are obviously in different parts of the world different levels of awareness, social and political development, cultural attitudes towards women. But just as the young churches are entirely justified in seeking to incarnate the expression of their faith in the prevailing culture of their countries, so the older churches need to apply themselves to the same task of inculturation. We cannot afford to ignore what the Spirit is saying in contemporary society as well as in the Church. It is important for us to discern and to baptise what is genuinely human. And so the local church and conferences of bishops should be appreciative of the particular charisms and contribution of women. In our own situations we should be willing, indeed eager, to recognise the role of women in the life of the Church and its decision-making processes. As far as ministry is concerned I would urge that there should be free and equal access of women to non-ordained ministries. The re-examination of 'Ministeria Quaedam' should take account of the experience of local churches.

In conclusion may I suggest that the issues of ministry and ministers are not remote from the daily experience of the Church and certainly not peripheral to its concerns. They are concerned intimately with our understanding of what it means to be the Church and with our sharing in Christ's mission to establish the kingdom of God. St Peter summed it up this way when he wrote:

As each has received a gift, employ it for one another, as good stewards of God's varied grace: whoever speaks, as one who utters oracles of God; whoever renders service, as one who renders it by the strength which God supplies; in order that in everything God may be glorified through Jesus Christ. To him belong glory and dominion for ever and ever. Amen. (1 Pet. 4:10–11)

5

The Age of the Laity

The Church, like Christ, is a sign of contradiction. In a world addicted to power, aggression and domination it stands for unconditional love and service of others. At a time when individual rights and human dignity are frequently ignored or trampled on it witnesses to the inalienable rights and absolute value of each individual. When society in general has turned its back on religious belief and practice the Church more than ever returns to the deepest mysteries and urges all its members to explore more profoundly the richness of God. In an age of anonymity and alienation the Church emphasises that individuals can find meaning and purpose in sharing the life and love of God himself.

Unbelief and secularism are rampant, yet at the same time the whole Church gives evidence of faith and vitality. A renewed understanding of scripture, theology and liturgy is leading to a fresh awareness of the inmost nature of the Church and of its mission and ministry. In turn this highlights the sublime calling of all the baptised, the overwhelming majority of whom are laity engaged in the daily life and work of the world. Some see ours as pre-eminently the age of the laity. Certainly the years since the Second Vatican Council have seen an abundance of new life and community building inspired and led by the laity in different parts of the world. The vocation and mission of the laity in the Church and in the world formed the theme of the 1987 International Synod of

Bishops in Rome. It provided an opportunity to assess how far the process of self-discovery and renewal has progressed in the two decades since the Second Vatican Council. Being Church in today's world involves laity directly and immediately. Yet the laity can be seen only in the context of the whole Church's life and mission.

Pope John Paul II made this clear at the Mass which concluded the 1987 Synod. He stressed that the laity bring to the Church precisely their secularity; their involvement in the life of the world is not irrelevant but essential to their vocation. He said:

> The Church, in the words of Pope Paul VI on the Council, 'has an authentic secular dimension, inherent in her intimate nature and mission, the root of which is to be found in the mystery of the Word incarnate and which is realised in diverse ways in her members'. The realisation of this secular dimension, of itself common to all the baptised, is brought about in a particular way by the faithful laity. The Council called it their 'secular nature'; the faithful laity 'live in the world, in each and all of the secular professions and occupations, and in the ordinary circumstances of family and social life, from which the very web of their existence is woven' (LG. 31). In this way they collaborate in the realisation of the total mission of the Church, which is not only to bring to men the message and grace of Christ but also to penetrate and perfect the temporal sphere with the Spirit of the Gospel. (AA. 5).

These words reveal the gap of understanding between the Church's own view of itself and its mission and that commonly held by so many people in Britain today. In the Church's vision love and service of God are not at odds with daily life, the joys and stresses of everyday living. There are not two separate planes of existence and operation; the spiritual and the mundane. Clergy and religious are not otherworldly while the bulk of laity remains inescapably in this world. The call to holiness and the call to justice are part of a single vocation. To appreciate the depth and sublimity of the laity's role in the Church it is necessary yet again to look at the way in which of recent years the Church has reaffirmed the basic insights of the Second Vatican Council.

The 1987 Synod on the Laity can be understood only in context. It has to be seen together with the Extraordinary Synod of 1985 and in light of the Second Vatican Council. There was a quite extraordinary anticipation and foreboding before the Extraordinary Synod. Media commentators tended to the belief that it had been called to turn back the clock to pre-Council days. It became in fact a celebration and verification of the Council. In a dramatic fashion the bishops of the world said 'yes' to Vatican II. Every president of every bishops' conference round the world attended that synod and each affirmed: 'Yes, in spite of the difficulties, we are on the right lines.' That was a significant moment in the contemporary history of the Church. We affirmed all that the Council had achieved some twenty years before and we laid particular stress on the four Constitutions seen now as the pillars of the Council: on the Church, on its role in the modern world, on liturgy and the Word of God. In these four documents are contained the seeds of new life for the Church. They probe its inner mystery; they outline its agenda for the transformation and sanctification of the world; they celebrate the source and summit of its life; they point to the Word of God revealed in scripture and tradition as the sure guide for its ongoing pilgrimage.

Another way of putting it is to say, perhaps a little simplistically, that acceptance of the four Constitutions help one to understand: what the Church 'is'; what it 'does'; what it 'thinks'; how it 'prays'.

To have affirmed the Council so decisively can be seen as an important stage in the reception of the Council by the Church. Avery Dulles, in his assessment of the Extraordinary Synod, analysed its Final Report and the principles it enunciated for the interpretation of the Council. He paraphrased them:

1. Each passage and document of the Council must be interpreted in the context of the others, so that the integral meaning of the Council may be rightly grasped.
2. The four major constitutions of the Council are the

hermeneutical key for the other decrees and declarations.

3. The pastoral import of the documents may not be separated from, or set in opposition to, their doctrinal content.

4. No opposition may be made between the spirit and the letter of Vatican II.

5. The Council must be interpreted in continuity with the great tradition of the Church, including earlier councils.

6. Vatican II must be accepted as illuminating the problems of our day. (*The Reception of Vatican II*, ed. Giuseppe Alberigo, CVAP, p. 350)

Here can be seen clearly the significance of the Extraordinary Synod for the interpretation of the Council and for the light it sheds on the 1987 Synod. Fr Dulles believes that in 1985 there emerged two schools: the 'neo-Augustinian' emphasising worship, holiness, separation from the world, internal coherence and unity on the one hand, and the 'communitarian' devoted to peace, justice and reconciliation on the other. The first group, he claims, used 'mystery' as a kind of code-word; the second group 'communion'. The first were eschatological and otherworldly; the second incarnational and this-worldly. I would agree with him that the Extraordinary Synod clearly acknowledged the emerging significance of the concept of koinonia or communion but I do not see that this in any way diminished the importance of 'mystery' or is alien to it. Both are essential in understanding the Church and the vocation and mission of the laity.

Until the Second Vatican Council the dominant ecclesiology or way of thinking about the Church was, on the whole, structural and institutional. Although the encyclical of Pope Pius XII on the Mystical Body broke new ground in papal teaching, we still tended to think of the Church largely in terms of the perfect society, visible, hierarchical, juridical. The image which most naturally suited this concept was that of the pyramid, ascending from the broad base of non-ordained laity, through various layers of hierarchical structure, reaching its apex in the Pope from whom flowed downwards all authority, teaching, ministry and mission. No doubt this is an oversimplification bordering on caricature. Some elements in this picture are largely derived historically from secular models but we must never forget that others in fact witness to essential truths about the hierarchical character of the Church. In trying to correct the images in people's minds we must never displace one misapprehension by another. The truth is, however, that the popular pyramidical understanding of the Church contained several inadequacies which in turn affected the laity's own appreciation of its role.

Implicit in an excessively structural and hierarchical model of the Church is the misapprehension that in some way there are first- and second-class citizens in God's kingdom and that laity are largely perceived to be, as it were, a passive supporting cast called on to stage when needed by the hierarchy, who are, and always remain, the principal protagonists in the mission of the Church. The role of the laity, in a famous phrase, is 'to pray, pay and obey'. Even bishops, in this overstated ecclesiology, were allotted a subsidiary, dependent role. In secular terms they were seen by some as little more than branch managers.

The Church, as perfect society, was seen by many to represent the sacred in direct confrontation with the secular which was regarded as essentially alien. This dualism, unconsciously Manichaean, tended to cast laity in an exclusively church-centred role or to see them as 'missionaries' sent out from the city of God into a hostile world. Sanctity was bound up closely with renunciation, a flight from the marketplace into the desert. The laity, devoted to their families and engaged in their daily work, could be forgiven for imagining that they had settled for 'second best'.

That set of assumptions, many of which were contrary to much in Catholic tradition and belief, finds no support in the Second Vatican Council. The emphasis of the Council was on the Church as mystery. This has nothing to do with the notion of puzzle, of the inexplicable. Mystery means instead an endlessly rich and unfolding truth which our unaided powers of reason could never have discovered but which leads us ever more deeply into the life and love of God, which is endless, infinite and ultimately beyond our individual comprehension. To guide our exploration into the mystery of the

Church the Council proposed a return to those biblical images we find in the first chapter of the Constitution on the Church. In recent years since the Council the concept of communion or koinonia, rooted in scripture, is found best able to lead into a truer understanding of that unity and diversity in the Church which mirrors and shares the inner life and love of the Trinity. It expresses something of the intimacy which exists with God and between all the baptised and which is the heart of the mystery that is the Church. New images are needed to express the reality of that community.

It has to be admitted, of course, that all our attempts to express the inexpressible are at best approximations. The Church is unique and has to be explained by means of analogies. It is 'like'; and it is also always 'unlike'. So images are to be employed with due caution.

To come closer to the reality of the Church we should think perhaps in terms of circle rather than of pyramid. Some prefer the image of a wheel whose spokes lead into and emerge out of the hub, which is Christ represented by his vicar who may be the pope, the bishop or the priest who shares his ministry, depending upon which manifestation of the Church we are considering.

Again one might think of interlocking circles as better approximating to the reality of the Christian community. The parish brings together smaller basic communities whose believers are gathered in the name of Christ. It becomes a community of communities. The particular church, the diocese, brings together round the bishop those local expressions of Church and each bishop with his diocese forms a single organic unity centred on the successor of St Peter, the pope. At each stage and manifestation of Church the body of Christ is made present and active, is whole and entire, yet is not divided or multiplied. Here language and imagery fail to convey the inmost truth. I suspect that there is a mystical truth here, a correlation between the eucharistic and ecclesial mystery of Christ. Just as the body of Christ is everywhere present in the Eucharist, yet is never multiplied or divided, so that body of Christ which is the Church is wholly present both here and throughout the world without confusion or multiformity.

This glimpse into mystery should convince us of the folly of applying political or sociological criteria to the Church. The vocation and role of the laity is not to be seen in terms of democracy or power-sharing. The truth is deeper and richer than that.

There is a fundamental equality and dignity among all men and women which springs from the creation itself. Scripture assures us that God has no favourites. He loves with his whole self and irrevocably all that he has made. Every human being is made by God in his own image and likeness. Each is uniquely willed and wanted by God and each manifests something of the truth and beauty of God which no one else can. On this, in the Judaeo-Christian vision, is based respect for the absolute dignity and rights of each individual and for the sanctity and inviolability of each human life. On this too is based the conviction that God calls each individual without exception to an ever more sublime destiny.

Human solidarity meant that the whole family of mankind was plunged into darkness and death by disobedience and sin. The second Adam, our Lord Jesus Christ, is light and life. In him the human is reconciled with the divine; all creation is afforded new hope, a new life, endless love. Baptism lifts us to new heights, makes us in a new and unique way partakers of the divine nature. We become brothers and sisters of Christ and temples of the Holy Spirit. We are in Christ and he in us. That is the fundamental equality and dignity to which we are all called in the Church. All the baptised share that single life, the one vocation, the same mission and ministry which is Christ's. Individually and equally we are called in baptism to share Christ's anointing as prophet, priest and king. Within that single body, as we have seen elsewhere, there is a variety of gifts and a distinction of roles and forms of service to enable the body to grow and be effective. Many of those ministries belong to the laity; some are entrusted solely to those of the baptised set aside for them by priestly and episcopal ordination. There is baptismal equality but a clear distinction of role consequent on ordination.

As far as the laity is concerned we are only at the beginning of the renewal which this understanding of the Church requires. Anyone involved in teaching or pastoral care of any

kind knows how self-image and expectations determine behaviour and achievement. If laity are to play their full part in
the life of the Church and to transform the world as they
should, then they have to come to realise the true nature and
scale of their calling in Christ. There has to be a new emphasis
on a somewhat forgotten feature of the Council's teaching
on the Church, namely the universal call to holiness and
especially how this affects lay people as they go about their
everyday duties. There have to be sustained and well-
prepared efforts to explain and commend to everyone the
reasons behind reform of the liturgy. There is an urgent and
crucial need for the active and informed participation of all
the faithful not only in the liturgy but in the mission and
ministry of the Church. People have to see how sharing in the
mission and ministry flows from and is inspired by sharing in
the liturgy. To be absolutely realistic and yet at the same time
deeply theological, there can be no renewal of the Church, no
revitalisation of the laity without unceasing attention to the
way we celebrate and take our full and proper share in the
parish Sunday Mass. It is precisely here that we are most
intensely and uniquely Church; it is here that we draw energy
for our daily task in the world.

I lay stress on this point because there are many admirable
projects for apostolate and formation which are not primarily
based on the parish community. To some extent they will not
succeed if they do not touch the believing and worshipping
Christian community where it gathers and when it gathers, in
the parish church on Sunday.

The renewed understanding of what it means to be Church
has given new and enriched significance to the local church of
the parish and also to the particular church which is the
grouping of the diocese around its bishop. It sheds light as
well on how both the ordained priesthood and the laity in
their different ways share Christ's ministry. I have already
spoken of collaborative ministry but I am conscious of how
little experience has yet been gained of this kind of sharing.
Undoubtedly there will be difficulties. New developments
will need prior consultation and careful explanation. In the
past reforms have failed of their full effect because of hasty
introduction and inadequate preparation.

This leads to a wider reflection which affects every attempt to renew the life of the Church in our day. To some extent, although it is early as yet to be sure, efforts to inspire people and institutions seem to fail because insufficient attention is paid to present reality, to where people are. We appeal to ideas and insights which create no echo in people's minds. No renewal of the Church, no fresh understanding, is possible without a better awareness of the mystery of the Trinity and of the theology of creation. Insufficient attention has been paid to both in the recent past.

Perhaps the way forward could be found in an attempt to integrate more fully the vision of Lumen Gentium with that of the other great Constitution, the Church in the Modern World, *Gaudium et Spes*. The Church is never to be thought of as self-sufficient, self-explanatory, existing in a vacuum. It exists in a real world; it lives and works for the whole world. Christ did not come to save the Church but the world. The Church which is his abiding presence shares his mission to reconcile all creation with the Father, to restore the unity of creation shattered by sin, to offer to the Father all renewed creation in one perfect sacrifice of praise, love, trust and obedience.

In a word it is the task of the whole Church at all times and in every part of the world to make this redemption a reality. It is all-absorbing and all-embracing. All members of the Church, and particularly the laity, in their daily life, work and relationships must be concerned to mend a broken world, to harness the world's resources to their proper and positive ends and to create a just, peaceful and caring society fit for children of God. They are stewards of God's creation. This is an immense responsibility and not just one tacked on to the spiritual and personal concerns which many consider to be the only proper task of the Church. All the baptised have a role to play in this mission in the world, the ordained no less than the laity. It has to be seen as holy and God-centred.

The Council's Decree on the Laity states quite clearly what should be the role of the laity in the world:

Christ's redemptive work has as its main objective the salvation of men, but it involves as well a reconstruction of the whole temporal order. Therefore the Church has been sent, not only to tell men about Christ and bring them his grace, but also to fill every corner of the world with the spirit of the Gospel and so bring it to its full perfection. The lay people, as they set about accomplishing this mission of the Church, work as apostles both in the Church and out in the world, among spiritual realities and among the things of our world. For even if there is a difference between these two, the spiritual and the transient, in the one and only plan of God they are so bound together that it is the whole universe that he intends to bring back to himself creating afresh in Christ. The beginnings of this new creation are here and now on earth, its final achievement awaits the last day. In both spheres, spiritual and transient, the lay person who is simultaneously a believer and a person in the world should be guided always by a Christian conscience which is at one with itself. (AA. N.5)

At the Synod on the Laity there was real recognition of the positive aspects of the laity's vocation and mission. Before any distinction of ministries and roles there is clearly recognised a single call to all the baptised to share in Christ's mission in the world. There are recognisably different ways of service within the Church but no grading into full-time and part-time Christians, into the committed and partly committed.

Language often reveals unspoken attitudes. Conscious affirmation of the laity is sometimes belied by official terminology and classification. In the new Code of Canon Law there are good descriptions of the laity but they tend to be negative on the lines that 'the laity are non-clergy and non-religious'. It reminds me somewhat of the category of female saints who formerly appeared in the Breviary as 'neither virgin nor martyr'. Since the laity constitute some 98.2 per cent of the people of God, it seems somewhat unreal to describe them as non-clergy. But it does indicate an attitude which must surely change under the pressure of new understanding. Their vocation and role must be accorded proper recognition and respect. They are vital to the Church's mission in the world.

In the twenty years which have elapsed since the Second Vatican Council new perceptions and preoccupations have emerged. There has been, for example, a quite definite advance into a post-colonial world amid an awakening of a sense of national identity and cultural autonomy in many Third World countries. The idea of inculturation, the rooting of the Christian revelation and worship in non-European forms, is a development beyond Vatican II, which never addressed itself to the issue. It poses many problems for the Church especially in discerning what cultural forms are compatible with the genius of the Gospel. Since in the next millennium the majority of Catholics will be found in the Third World this has become an urgent issue. Since the Second Vatican Council there have undoubtedly been changes in the way the laity see their role in the Church. In Britain there has been a marked decline in the numerical strength of the mainstream lay organisations. More energy and enthusiasm has been directed towards single-issue campaigns such as pro-life, justice and peace. And there is evidence of more widespread involvement by laity in the life and witness of the local parish and in ecumenical activity at local level. The Catholic laity too, perhaps as a result not as much of the Second Vatican Council but of a successful system of Catholic schools, has become a more visible and influential component in the life of the nation. They make their individual contribution in every sector. That too is part of being Church in today's world.

We have not experienced anything in Britain to compare with the radical enthusiasm of the basic communities and the vigour and involvement of the new movements now so evident especially in Mediterranean Europe. I have already considered at some length the contribution of the basic communities but not enough is known about the new movements as yet in this country to form anything more than general impressions. The 1987 Synod Fathers extended to them a cautious welcome. It was remarkable that almost no lay representatives at that synod came from the kind of parish-based lay organisations so familiar to us in Britain. There was a virtual eclipse of the old Cardijn movements, the YCW, YSC and Catholic Worker Groups. I find it impossible to believe that none of these has anything creative to offer to Catholic laity today.

Certainly the post-conciliar period has seen the rise of some high-profile, well-organised and deeply committed groups such as Comunione e Liberazione, the Neo-Catechumenate, and others. They display admirable energy and idealism and are no doubt prompted by the Holy Spirit. There is some concern among the bishops however that the movements should respect episcopal authority and diocesan and national pastoral plans. When a movement is imported from abroad there is an obvious need for its leaders to sit down with local bishops to see what modifications are needed in its pastoral methods. Especially if a movement involves itself in public affairs there is even greater need for local discernment and guidance. Lay organisations have to respect the structure and dynamic of the Church itself.

Since the laity by their very vocation are responsible for the restoration of all things in Christ it is not surprising that they are faced constantly with questions about the relation between religion and life, Church and state, politics and the Gospel. In Chapter 12 I try to provide some answer to these questions. They tend to be answered differently in Britain than elsewhere. At an international gathering like the 1987 Synod it was remarkable how widespread and insistent was the demand that the Church as a whole should play its full part in public life and that Church members, guided by their convictions, should be involved in the political process. Great stress was placed on the responsibility of Christians for the world around them. There is obvious and urgent need for both individual and collective action to build a society that is more just, peaceful and authentically human. No doubt these convictions arise from bitter experience of degradation, corruption and tyranny.

In many parts of the world the Church is confronted with struggle and repression. Few countries have known long periods of independence, freedom and stability. In many places the Church, the people of God, represents the only coherent force standing for human rights and individual dignity. In the countries of the First World too, the Church is sometimes rebuked for its social conscience. Yet its religious vision compels it to speak out for the poor, the unborn, the unemployed, the handicapped, those pushed to the margins of society.

It is wrong to spiritualise the role and mission of the laity in a way that leaves the daily world of work, politics, economics, family life and leisure to other less benign forces. Here is a task to engage in different ways all the baptised, ordained and lay alike. It is altogether too simplistic and unreal to define, as it were, spheres of influence and to allot the inner spiritual life of the Church to clergy and religious while consigning secular life and its concerns exclusively to the laity. The collaborative ministry to which I have already referred requires a proper and balanced partnership of clergy and laity in both Church and world, with, of course, a differentiation of roles. There is a single mission; there are different functions and forms of service. So-called 'privatised' religion has no foundation in scripture or the social teaching of the Church. That commits all of us to the building of the kingdom in the city of man.

6

The Call to Holiness

Most people would like to be thought of as good but would be embarrassed at being called holy. That suggests that there is something amiss with our notion of holiness. It should be central to our Christian conviction about ourselves and the world God continues to create. In biblical terms we are all called to be holy. Indeed the reason for our recurring unhappiness is that we so often fail to be holy and thereby frustrate God's loving designs in our regard. Holiness is for everyone and needs to be universally understood and desired.

Perhaps because of misapprehensions the chapter in the Council's Constitution on the Church entitled 'A Universal Call to Holiness' has not been given the emphasis it deserves. Holiness should be seen as the authentic individual way to live the mystery of Church. If the concept were properly defined, it would also be immediately obvious that in every age holiness is always the key to renewal of life and love in all human activity. After all, the call to holiness by the Church echoes the words of our Lord himself when he proclaimed, 'repent and believe in the gospel' (Mark 1:14).

There can be no holiness without this fundamental conversion. It involves a decisive turning away from all that separates us from God, in a word, from sin, and a turning towards God, to listen to him attentively and to obey him faithfully. This is the change of heart, the metanoia for which our Lord called. It is not a single, once for all, decision but a state of mind and a commitment of life that is constantly affirmed and renewed. It becomes, with God's abiding help, the way we think and act. Daily we die to ourselves and live to God and live in God.

The call to this new way of life is not confined to a select few. It is made to anyone who would follow Christ. It invites each of us to rise above the mediocre and the lukewarm to the very heights. As Christ said: 'You, therefore, must be perfect, as your heavenly Father is perfect' (Matt. 5:48). Lest anyone seek exemption the Second Vatican Council insisted: 'It is clear then that all of Christ's faithful, no matter what their rank or station, have a vocation to the fullness of the Christian life and the perfection of charity' (LG. 40). The call to holiness then, is addressed impartially to bishop, priest, layperson and religious, but to avoid ambiguity I want to stress that in what follows I wrote throughout with lay people principally in mind.

When Jesus Christ called his hearers to repentance he urged them to believe in the Gospel. That would set out for them a whole new way of life. At the heart of the Gospel is the twofold commandment: 'You shall love the Lord your God with all your heart, and with all your soul, and with all your strength, and with all your mind; and your neighbour as yourself' (Luke 10:27). To live this love leads to true holiness. In fact holiness is well defined as living in a radical way the commandment to love God and my neighbour. It gives unity and purpose to every life.

Inevitably this will make great demands on us. To love in the Gospel sense means to devote one's energies to, make one's own, the concerns that are God's. This runs counter, too often, to our natural instincts and preferences. Holiness requires a spirit of obedience to the will of God and a willing acceptance of it. It involves one's whole self in a generous service of others. This has nothing to do with what personally appeals or satisfies. In fact an acid test of true holiness is whether one perseveres in faithfulness to God even when everything seems to suggest that God either does not care or does not exist. It is also genuine holiness to put oneself out in the service of those who are uncongenial or not particularly sympathetic. I suspect that genuinely holy people set out to serve others cheerfully and in the process find they begin to feel some affection for them, and not the other way round.

Few, I suppose, spend much time reflecting on aspects of holiness so it might help to focus more closely on some of them. Usually conversion is not a sudden, unexpected, overwhelming experience as it was, for example, in the case of St Paul on the road to Damascus. For most, instead, it is a gradual growth in holiness. It involves a constant turning away from sin and embracing of Gospel values. It is a lifelong task, taking time and much patient effort. In all probability it will include many failures. Perhaps it might help to recall a saying I have seen attributed to Sir Winston Churchill that success is never final and failure is never fatal. Fear of failure can be a crippling handicap.

Not the mere fact of failure but being able to recognise and accept it is part of the process of growing to be holy. For many of us failure is the only way to develop a healthy humility and that is the essential foundation of true holiness. Arrogance and pride are clear indications of its absence. The process of achieving humility is painful and no one is ever entirely and finally successful. Yet every attempt to become more humble helps us realise how dependent we are on God and how without him we are literally nothing. We do not even become holy by our own efforts; God makes us holy. His love is the source of all; his creative energy sustains and enlivens all.

Much frustration, anxiety and distortion could be avoided if only we recognised at all times that the initiative always rests with God even when we are convinced that we are solely responsible. Whatever we do and achieve is always in response to his action and that is still the case when we are least aware of it.

We need encouragement if we are to play our part by cooperating with God's action. We remain free, after all, to refuse to cooperate or we can simply drift away. Fear can sometimes be salutary and on occasion forms the only starting point for conversion but growth in holiness can never be fostered long by fear. Instead we need to take fresh heart by meditating constantly on God's unchanging and boundless love for us. I recommend the words of Isaiah: 'Can a woman forget her sucking child, that she should have no compassion on the son of her womb? Even these may forget, yet I will not forget you. Behold, I have graven you on the palms of my hands' (Isa. 49:15–16). And then Chapter 15 of St Luke's Gospel is a source of endless encouragement. These two passages, and there are many more in scripture, help us understand what St John meant when he wrote that God is love (1 John 4:8).

Holiness is thus bound up with a life of love for God, oneself and neighbour. It would be folly to try to divide one from the other or, worse, to set them in opposition. Later I hope to show that spiritual maturity is achieved with the growing realisation that God is in all things and all things are in God, including one's own self. It is a false dualism that seeks to sunder love of God from love of neighbour, that despises or hates one's own being and fails to recognise the unity of all creation in the Word through whom all things are made.

Basically it is this same insight which enables us to realise that holiness is not something extraneous or extraordinary but has to be achieved where we are and in and through the circumstances and experiences of our daily lives. The Council taught this clearly: 'all Christ's faithful will grow daily more holy in the conditions their life imposes, its duties and its circumstances' (LG. 41). This is a basic truth about our search for God and about our sharing his life and love. It is uniquely Christian and yet not widely appreciated even by those who profess a belief in Christ. It is important to reflect on three fundamental principles.

The first is that we operate as God's stewards in the very place where we are. We are made in the image of God the Creator and all our human activity is the working out of God's creative act. The first two chapters of Genesis vividly witness to the kinship of mankind with all creation and the entrusting of all living and growing things into the care of the human race. We are naturally creative in all we do. G. K. Chesterton once wrote that art is the signature of man. Human technology and the achievements of mankind in so many fields bear witness to fertile minds and immense energies. We are co-creators with God of new life and we help to nurture and bring to maturity the children of the next generation. In some sense all we do is part of the ongoing act of divine creation. Only when we sin or refuse to live and work in accordance with God's will do we fail to share God's creativity. That failure disfigures creation.

The second principle is that, since God became man in Jesus Christ, all human activity now has a quite special meaning and significance. Human life and work have been irrevocably sanctified and made significant by the coming of God into our flesh and our history. Through Christ all humanity has been lifted up and can now share the gift of divine life and love. As Christ, our brother, pleased his Father throughout his life and in his death, we too can give glory to God by our lives and death as his children.

Thirdly, we can learn much from the obvious fact that God made man spent by far the greater part of his short life in the seclusion and obscurity of a hill village in Galilee, content with the daily round of family life, work and prayer. That hidden and almost private life in Nazareth is immensely significant and important. It reveals the power and the beauty of everyday ordinary living; God is present there, lives and loves there just as surely as among the great and the powerful. Jesus must have helped to keep the home at Nazareth tidy, have played with other children when he was a child, and done many of the things which we may judge to be routine and unimportant.

Spiritual writers, reflecting throughout the centuries on the meaning of the incarnation and redemption, have distilled for us so much that is of the utmost importance for our contemporary living.

We can learn much even amid adversity and hardship. The Second Vatican Council said that people will grow in holiness 'if they combine their faith with an acceptance of everything which comes from the hand of their heavenly Father' (LG. 41). Every priest can normally point to someone in his experience who manifests unconquerable faith and trust in God despite bereavement, injustice, poverty, sickness. It seems folly to remain free and trusting when all goes wrong but faith in Christ demands acceptance of his words: 'If any man would come after me, let him deny himself and take up his cross and follow me' (Matt. 16:24). Sometimes God seems to impose impossible burdens on his 'special friends'.

That phrase recalls vividly to mind my visit to Ethiopia at the height of the famine in November 1984. In one of the camps, amid the thousands of starving people, I met an English Vincentian nun over eighty years old. She pulled me to one side insisting that I accompany her to a tumbledown hut where, she said, her 'special friends' were to be found. She took me with such evident love to the side of people who were not only dying of starvation but were also blind, crippled and utterly helpless. They had nothing human to commend them but she saw in them the face of Christ in his agony and I saw in her the face of the compassionate Christ.

Many people experience ill-health, depression, misfortunes of one kind or another. Some are tempted to doubt the love of God or even his very existence but that is to deny that every life must encounter its share of sorrow and to miss its significance for our human growth. Only the believer in Christ has light and faith enough to begin to grasp something of what St Paul wrote on the mystery of pain:

> For the word of the cross is folly to those who are perishing, but to us who are being saved it is the power of God . . . For Jews demand signs and Greeks seek wisdom, but we preach Christ crucified, a stumbling block to Jews and folly to Gentiles, but to those who are called, both Jews and Greeks, Christ the power of God and the wisdom of God. For the foolishness of God is wiser than men, and the weakness of God is stronger than men . . . God chose what is low and despised in the world, even things that are not, to bring to nothing things that are, so that no human being might boast in the presence of God. He is the source of your life in Christ Jesus, whom God made our wisdom, our righteousness and sanctification and redemption. (1 Cor. 1:18, 22–25, 28–30)

The wisdom resplendent in these words has been understood by many people who may not be particularly versed in scripture or well read in academic terms but whose lives and hearts have been touched and healed by Christ. They are our teachers. I never visit a hospital ward or encounter people whose strong faith sustains them in poverty and adversity without returning humbled and edified.

Suffering has a key role in the growth of personal holiness. It detaches from worldly goods and achievements. It sharpens our understanding of what is really important and significant and puts things in a truer perspective. It points us beyond this world to a fulfilment which is final and all-satisfying and where we find our lasting home.

In the Christian understanding of life's purpose, we learn to recognise that nothing is too small for God. He loves every scrap, every second of all that he has made. He intends the human mind and heart to rejoice and give thanks and appreciate his presence in all that is. Every human act can be an act of love, a response to the Love that gave us everything.

A consequence of this which is of the utmost importance for our growth in holiness is the awareness that all life is holy and that we meet God in each and every moment. God is now, and the present moment can be seen as a sacrament, a sign and effective symbol of our constant encounter with him. We meet God in the present moment: the past is gone, the future is not yet but here and now – in every 'now' – we can be at one in thought and action with God.

The habit of short quick prayers, the frequent focusing of our thoughts, enables us to sense the presence of God. It is a mutually reinforcing process. The habit of such prayers helps us acquire the sense of his presence; the sense of his presence prompts the prayer and the fleeting thought.

I make no apology for looking at the growth of personal holiness in what some might regard as a very traditional manner. The fundamental principles of holiness are always contemporary without being subject to the dictates of fashion. Some, I realise, will criticise what I have written so far, on the grounds that the holiness described is too individualistic and personal. Again I make no apologies for that. Whatever we believe and rightly say about the communitarian aspect of the Christian life, we cannot ever deny the need for personal faith, conversion and commitment and for the close relationship which has to be developed between God and each individual. God indwells the inner self of the believer; the mystery of the transcendent God is encountered within. There is no other ground where that meeting takes place.

I am aware that others may say with some justification that much of what I have written so far suggests a degree of Pelagianism. They may object that I have placed too much emphasis on what the individual does. Yet I would maintain that in fact I have been talking all the time about openness to God and our willingness to let God be within us. I have tried to explain how we must cooperate with initiatives taken by God. There is a danger, of course, of thinking that all depends on 'me'. It does not. As we advance in holiness we realise the truth that outside God there is literally nothing. We come, often quite painfully, to acknowledge our utter dependence on God. In the Catholic spiritual tradition this is accompanied by an increasing appreciation of the significance and importance of the sacramental system and of each of the sacraments in turn as they are received and celebrated in the different stages and circumstances of life. For steady growth and nourishment, in particular, we recognise our dependence on the sacraments of Eucharist and reconciliation.

For all of us, the sacrament of penance or reconciliation is essential. It helps us, as sometimes wayward or stumbling pilgrims, to face up to the reality of ourselves, to acknowledge our frailty, and to recognise especially the need to say 'sorry' to God and be assured through the priest of our Father's prodigal love. Our sins may well have damaged others or have caused us to breach our relationships of justice and charity with them; the sacrament seals our repentance, admits us again to the fullness of fellowship. The Eucharist too is 'our daily bread', the absolutely indispensable nourishment of the body and blood of our blessed Lord. Through the Eucharist as sacrifice we are able to offer ourselves together with all that concerns us to the Father, in and with Christ, the eternal and all-sufficient sacrifice. The Eucharist as communion unites us to Christ so utterly and intimately that we live now no longer for ourselves but Christ lives in us (cf Gal. 2:20).

St Paul is often able to baffle and beguile. Two passages in the present context leave the reader fascinated but still in search of meaning. In the letter to the Galatians to which I have just referred, what exactly does he mean? 'I have been crucified with Christ; it is no longer I who live, but Christ who lives in me; and the life I now live in the flesh I live by faith in the Son of God, who loved me and gave himself for me' (Gal. 2:20). How am I to understand the presence of God within me? Do I cease to be myself? In what sense am I identified with the Christ who now is said to live in me? Is my sacrifice his as his is mine? Here we have reached mystery, a truth that we cannot really understand, let alone explain but one which nevertheless tantalises and thrills. Our identification is such that in us the Father sees the Son and is well pleased. He can never cease to love us absolutely and unceasingly in that infinite life and love which is the reality of the Triune God. Only our sin can disfigure the face of Christ, can be our free choice to turn our back on our Father and his house. But the father of the prodigal can never cease to love.

The second passage of St Paul occurs in his letter to the Colossians: 'If then you have been raised with Christ, seek the things that are above, where Christ is, seated at the right hand of God' (Col. 3:1). Baptism has transformed us. If we live by the life of Christ, that is already a life that is risen, ascended, glorified. We are now members of the family of God, brothers and sisters of Christ, children of the one Father, temples of the Holy Spirit. Indeed our lives in their inmost reality are 'hidden with Christ in God' (3:3). Consequently we are urged by Paul: 'Set your minds on things that are above, not on things that are on earth' (3:2). The life we lead on earth is to be radically different from that of unbelievers. We are to put to death what is earthly: 'fornication, impurity, passion, evil desire, and covetousness, which is idolatry' (3:5). We must put away 'anger, wrath, malice, slander, and foul talk' (3:8). We are not to lie to each other either and the reason for this new way of life is clear: 'you have put off the old nature with its practices and have put on the new nature, which is being renewed in knowledge after the image of its creator' (3:9–10). We have been reborn to a new life; in us, as in Christ, the image of God is being revealed in all its glory. Christ told Philip that those who saw him had already seen the Father. In an even more mysterious way the same is true of us. We are now 'God's chosen ones, holy and beloved' and are to put on 'compassion, kindness, lowliness, meekness, and patience, forbearing one another and, if one has a complaint against another, forgiving each other . . . And above all these put on love, which binds everything together in perfect harmony' (3:12–14).

Holiness springs from an individual's personal relationship with God but then has to relate to everything else in God since all in fact is in God. No individual remains isolated. We the baptised are members of Christ's body, sharing one life and so are mutually interdependent. We are each part of that communio, that living fellowship, whereby we share in the very life of the Trinity, growing in knowledge and love through the scriptures and the sacraments.

In this mystery of life and love, in a way we do not fully comprehend, the sinfulness and spiritual sickness of one individual affects the whole just as the holiness and health of one has also its effect on all. We are in very truth members of each other; the living body of Christ brings into unity all those who have found faith in him: together, as redeemed humanity, we make our way back to the Father.

7

Thoughts on Spirituality

The first book known to have been written by a woman in English is acknowledged throughout the world as a spiritual classic. 'The Revelations of Divine Love' by Mother Julian of Norwich is the fruit of long meditation on a series of sixteen 'shewings' of our Lord which Julian experienced during a severe illness in May 1373. One of the best-known passages from her Revelations provides a starting-point for my reflections on spiritual life today:

He shewed me a little thing, the size of a hazelnut, in the palm of my hand, and it was as round as a ball. I looked at it with my mind's eye and I thought: what can this be? And answer came: it is all that is made. I marvelled that it could last for I thought it might have crumbled to nothing, it was so small. And the answer came into my mind, 'It lasts and ever shall because God loves it'. And all things have being through the love of God.

In this little thing I saw three truths. The first is that God made it. The second is that God loves it. The third that God looks after it.

What is he indeed that is maker and lover and keeper? I cannot find words to tell. For until I am one with him I can never have true rest nor peace. I can never know it until I am held so close to him that there is nothing in between.

'It lasts and ever shall because God loves it' – here we can start
our search for God and reflect on how best to satisfy in our day
that ceaseless hunger and thirst for God that springs from our
very nature. We are made in the image and likeness of God
and there is in each of us a yearning – consciously recognised
or not – for the Father and source of our being. Each one of us
is so much more precious than the hazelnut. That thought
alone encourages an exploration into the mystery of love
which God is.

Mother Julian recognised that all things are made and loved
and looked after by God. It is this that leads us to long
unceasingly for God and to be restless until united with him.
Yet contemporary society has convinced itself that it has
largely outgrown the need for God. It boasts of being post-
Christian. It is quite confident that, given time and the
inevitability of technological progress, all problems can be
solved and all mystery eliminated from life. This is a state of
mind which is not so much hostile to Christian revelation and
to the life of the spirit as indifferent to them, dismissing them
as irrelevant. Many people simply fail to recognise the foundations on which their own society and its culture are based.
They fail to appreciate the heritage of shared attitudes,
values, laws and institutions they have inherited from their
Christian forebears.

And yet it is impossible to eliminate God from human
consciousness, and difficult to deny his presence in history.
On the contrary, it is possible to argue that most of the
prevailing preoccupations of modern and secularised society
are in fact echoes of the Christian Gospel preached to the
world over the centuries. Women's liberation, concern for the
Third World, thirst for justice and equality, work for peace
and a vision of the global village and a single human family
can all be traced back to the Gospel and reflect kingdom-
values.

This is not unimportant. We are not living in a world devoid
of hope and divorced from God. We may be buffeted by the
prevailing winds of unbelief. We may suffer from society's
generalised distrust of organised religion and Church structures. But at the same time there is still to be found in
unexpected places a persistent thirst for God and for the life

of the Spirit, a certain longing for prayer and meditation and a curiosity about all forms of religious experience.

There remains the inner restlessness of the human spirit and its ceaseless search for meaning and fulfilment. Individuals are thus kept open to the possibility of God and receptive to the Spirit. These are echoes of God deep within us.

A lot of people today are, I believe, ready to accept a deeper, more genuine understanding of who they are, of their ultimate meaning. But there remains the problem of how to awaken in people generally an awareness of their human condition and of how to help them in this search for meaning. The majority of people, in practice, do not analyse their situation in any depth but simply remain dissatisfied. They appreciate beauty and the wonders of nature but the innate longing for God which is always part of themselves tends to be dissipated in pursuit of limited goals and disorganised values. They go in search of many false gods, having failed in practice to perceive the uniqueness and necessity of the one true God. To awaken ourselves to the living reality of God and to walk alongside our contemporaries in their search for God, we need, I suggest, to adopt an approach which St Paul took when confronted with a similar situation and to ask of them and ourselves what Paul asked of the Athenians of his day.

Paul is recorded in Acts 17 as coming to Athens, the cultural capital of the ancient world. There he encountered the sophistication and diversity of classical paganism. At the same time, he was faced with a pluralism like that of our own day, an openness to new and foreign influences. As the author of Acts commented: 'The one amusement the Athenians and the foreigners living there seemed to have, apart from discussing the latest ideas, is listening to lectures about them' (Acts 17:21). Paul, throughout his missionary journeys, both proclaimed and persuaded. In Athens we see exemplified his technique of persuasion. He suggests an approach that we can ourselves adopt to learn more of God and lead others in search of that same knowledge. He lays foundations for a unique Christian spirituality based on an awareness of, and relationship with, the One who is both Other and at the same time our inmost reality. He recognises and gives thanks to

God for the unity and goodness of all creation. That spirituality helps us to hear, accept and celebrate the Good News that the Word incarnate has come to restore all to unity. It provides the rich soil in which the seed, which is the Word, can bear fruit 'some a hundredfold, some sixty, some thirty' (Matt. 13:8).

Standing in the middle of the Areopagus, St Paul pointed to the altar with the inscription: 'To an unknown God' (Acts 17:23). He explained that he had come to speak of that very same God. He is the creator who gives mankind its life and breath and everything it needs. He made humankind from a single stock so all nations might equally seek God 'in the hope that they might feel after him and find him' (17:27). Paul explains that 'he is not far from each one of us, for "in him we live and move and have our being"; as even some of your poets have said, "For we are indeed his offspring"' (17:28). He goes on to proclaim that God 'will judge the world in righteousness by a man whom he has appointed, and of this he has given assurance to all men by raising him from the dead' (17:31). He moves from where his audience is, from their religious sense and their feeling for creation into an exploration of the nature of God. He then confronts his audience with the unknown, with what challenged belief, with a revelation of the Word incarnate. It was a teaching which led some to turn from him as others had turned from Christ but which led some to a commitment of faith and entry into the Way, the Truth and the Life. It was an approach based on the conviction that there is but one revelation of God made manifest in our inner experience, in creation, in the coming of the Son of God.

People today, like the Athenians of old, thirst for the one who is still for many 'the unknown God'. The search for God should not be confined to the few. It is open to all. It is indeed necessary for all if they are ever to achieve health and lasting happiness. To become aware of God, to hear his word, to respond to him, to live in his light and in accordance with his will is no optional extra. It is a prerequisite for wholeness. Life in the Spirit is the only authentic means of responding to the mystery of ourselves and of our existence. It is not, therefore, the preserve of the religious elite, of those who give their entire lives to the service of God and his Church. It is a treasure to be found in the midst of daily life, in the home and family, at work, in all the activities of a busy and fulfilled life, in the pain and desolation of bereavement, sickness, handicap, loneliness. No matter where we are, in all the circumstances of our lives we can find God, experience his healing and presence and that joy and peace which the world cannot give. This is such an all-important element of life that we should do everything possible to develop it for ourselves and to share it with others.

The term 'spiritual life' is not in common use certainly among people today. They tend to talk instead of their prayer-life, or of formation, or of growing in their faith, or faith journey, of trying to get closer to Christ. Or they tend to focus on social action and concern for issues of justice and peace. The spiritual life includes all of those, indeed is the source from which all else flows:

> What then, is the spiritual life? It is that interior life whereby I strive to encounter God and develop my relationship with him by my becoming increasingly more aware of him and by desiring him more intensely. It is not something separate from the rest of my life, a part of me having no connection with anything else. The spiritual life involves all that I do, all that happens to me; all that I am; it should permeate every activity and be itself active at every moment. It is furthermore the reason for my service of God and neighbour. It is what makes me 'tick'. A spiritual life is simply a life in which all we do comes from the centre where we are anchored in God: a life soaked through and through by a sense of his reality and claim, and self-given to the great movement of his will. (Evelyn Underhill, *The Spiritual Life*)

How, then, do we become 'soaked through and through' by a sense of the reality of God? How do we become abandoned to the 'great movement of his will'? At the very centre of our being we must become conscious of his presence. There is a God-sized space within us, a former archbishop of Canterbury once wrote, which only God can fill. When he begins to fill that space, then we are, as it were, anchored in God.

There is then, in the human make-up a fundamental need for God. I would speak of a 'desiring' or a 'wanting' within us that can only be satisfied totally and finally when he, the real object of all our desiring, is possessed by us. There is too a restlessness of the mind, always in search of truth, for ultimate meaning, for knowledge and reasons. It will only be when all is known and love secure, that we shall be at rest. Indeed the fulfilment of all our knowing and wanting is that ecstasy of love which is union with the God who is all truth and who is, of all that is lovable, the most lovable of all. That experience of love totally fulfilled belongs to the future, to our being in another situation, where there will be nothing for any of us save the immediacy of the vision of God. It is something to which we rightly look forward.

Meanwhile we search and grope for some achieving of an 'awareness' of God and of his presence within us, and for our 'desiring' of him to be satisfied. To set out on that pilgrimage of discovery and search will involve, always, radical change within us, that metanoia or change of heart, which is involved when we turn to God or strive to let him into the centre of our being.

Where then do we begin to look to find God, or at least to catch a glimpse of him? Do we hear his voice calling to us or at any rate listen to the echo of his call? We do not, of course, see him as he truly is, nor do we hear his voice clear and compelling, like the call of a lover to the loved one. Moses had prayed 'show me thy glory' and he was told 'no one can see God and live'. Moses hid in the cleft in the rock and God covered him with his hand till he had passed by: 'I will take away my hand, and you shall see my back; but my face shall not be seen' (Exod. 33:23). We can see now only something of God, know him in his work, as the artist in his creation. We can listen to his word, the scriptures, written for us and passed down within the believing community from one generation to the next; we can find him too in those deep experiences of joy or pain which constitute his urgent call to us to draw closer to him. Above all there is his Word, the Word that became flesh 'the image of the invisible God, the first-born of all creation' (Col. 1:15).

In creation, in the scriptures, in Jesus Christ, we seek God and see something of him or hear the echo of his voice. We sense his presence outside ourselves. But at the very centre of our being, deep within us, his presence may be experienced as he becomes part of our awareness and the object of our desiring. We may indeed have a sense of his presence.

I find that phrase 'sense his presence' helpful. No words are ever adequate to describe what God is like; he cannot be contained in any image or idea, and our senses are clearly of no avail. None the less from the different words that he has spoken, whether it be in creation, in the scriptures or in his only begotten Son, we may construct our own idea or picture of him – inadequate, no doubt, childish and naïve maybe, but important for us as the only way we have of thinking about him and of allowing those thoughts to prompt our desiring.

We should note, however, that our desiring of God is not always, or even necessarily, dependent on our knowledge of him or on our awareness of his presence. Desiring can outstrip them both. To desire is a fundamental law of our being. We are attracted now by this good, now by that one, and only completely satisfied by that most perfect good of all, God himself. In other words we are made for love, and God is the only one that can still the craving of the human heart. We may 'crave' without being too certain what it is we so earnestly desire.

There is much more to the spiritual life than our attempt to become aware of the presence of God within us and the stirring of our desiring of him. But the awareness and the desiring are linked with our being 'soaked through and through by a sense of his reality and claim' and thus making it clear that, sinful though we may be, our duty is to yield to the demands which he undoubtedly makes upon us. God draws us to himself through our need for him, but there will come a point – and it is a sign of a maturer spiritual life – when we shall realise that God is not there to satisfy us, but that we are for him and exist to offer our worship and obedience.

I sometimes hear people speak of what the Church does or does not give to them, while others speak of what they feel they can contribute to the Church. These are admirable sentiments, and are to be encouraged. However we need to beware. 'I' and 'me' should never be at the centre of the stage.

God is. What he wants, what he claims, what he permits, what he demands – that is what matters most. Thus to make the point once more: we exist to please God; we must learn to forget ourselves. Is this not the meaning of losing our lives in order to find them?

Awareness of God and our longing for him, with the sense of his presence within us, and the slow realisation of what he demands from us, come normally from the consistent and regular practice of prayer. I say 'normally' because God's action can never be constrained by human activity or subordinated to it. Indeed we know from experience how active and very busy people can achieve great holiness; and this despite the fact that a lot of people live in cramped physical circumstances with little or no space for silence and solitude. They seem to have none of the advantages enjoyed by priests and religious. How then are they able to achieve an awareness of God and his love? I shall return to the point later. I would merely observe that there should be in everybody's life an attempt to find some space in the day for prayer, however brief. It is, I repeat, normally in prayer that our awareness of God and our desire are awakened.

What is prayer? This is not the place to present an exhaustive study of prayer. Let me just remind you of that simple definition of prayer as 'the raising of the mind and heart to God'. The key word is 'trying' – for to try in relation to the things of God is all that we can do – whatever achievement or success there may be is a gift from God. Time spent trying to pray, however unsuccessful it may seem to be, is time well spent. From that regular practice a sense of his presence becomes stronger, we become more aware of him and desire him more intensely. From that flow our actions of service towards God and our neighbour.

In our attempts to be in contact through prayer with God, we use on occasions words (prayers we recite or read); sometimes images (thinking about a scene in the Bible, for example); or again we reflect on an idea (for instance, God is merciful or good or loving). In each case our words, images or ideas are to lead us to the Person, Father, Son or Holy Spirit. Images and ideas as the product of our reflection lead us generally to considerations about God. We cannot get to God himself except in so far as he enables us to do so. Sometimes we get no further than the sense of a presence which is beyond words, images and ideas. It can be likened to being in a dark and silent room with a loved one, no words being spoken, no sight vouchsafed, just a sense of the presence of the other. These moments of 'presence' are gift from God, frequent for some, rare for others. Being gift they are neither of right nor reward. They are more likely to occur to one faithful in prayer and in life.

For many this talk of a sense of presence may well seem remote and unrealistic. Most of us live in a muddle, full of uncertainties and hesitations, with confused ideas of God, often haunted by feelings of guilt. For such, words addressed to God and thoughts about him mean little or nothing. If we are conscious of being in a state of grave sin, then we have good reason to feel abandoned and lost. The converse however is not true; that is, if we feel lost and abandoned it does not mean that we are in sin. God allows the experience in order to free us from wrong attachments and draw us to himself. It is good to feel futile before God and to wait patiently for him to find us. We may be deprived of the joy of sensing his presence, but we give to him the joy of our trusting him and especially when trust is given in the dark and without seeking reward. Love of God grows when faith is purified. When faith is purified there is darkness and often a terrible night of pain. These are precious moments when God will come to fill the space that he has fashioned for himself.

In 1987 I visited St Thérèsc's cell in the Carmel of Lisieux. By the door of her cell, scratched into the wood, she had written 'Jésus est mon unique amour'. That was not written in exaltation but in near despair. She was thus crying out to her beloved that even when she experienced nothing but absence, emptiness, darkness she clung to the assurance of being loved and carried in his arms. That is faith at a heroic level – that is trust, clinging to God when everything in our experience would seem to contradict his very existence or at least the fact of his love for us.

There are of course many roads that lead to God. It was St Paul, writing to the Romans, who taught that from the visible creation we should be able to learn about God: 'Ever since the creation of the world his invisible nature, namely, his eternal power and deity, has been clearly perceived in the things that have been made' (Rom. 1:20). The world in which we live speaks to us of God. The Book of Wisdom chapter 13 was clearly St Paul's source; but the meaning of both texts was clarified for me by a passage from C. S. Lewis's *Letters to Malcolm* when he wrote:

> I was learning the far more secret doctrine that pleasures are shafts of the glory as it strikes our sensibility. As it [that is, the glory] impinges on our wills or our understanding; we give it different names – goodness or truth or the like, but its flash upon our senses and mood is pleasure.

So music that charms the ear, the beauty of a landscape or of a person that pleases the eye, the glass of wine that delights the palate – these are all 'shafts of the glory of God', reminding us of his beauty which they mirror. The author of the Book of Wisdom warns us not to turn what should speak to us of God into idols, things we worship for their own sakes and do not value and cherish for his.

> If, charmed by their beauty, they have taken things for gods, let them know how much the Lord of these excels them, since the very Author of beauty has created them. And if they have been impressed by their power and energy, let them deduce from these how much mightier is he that has formed them, since through the grandeur and beauty of the creatures we may, by analogy, contemplate their Author. (Wisd. 13:3–5)

If we are aware of God's presence in creation and see in it a reflection of his goodness and beauty, then we become, surely, more aware too of the stewardship which has been entrusted to us, less likely to think in terms of a sharp distinction between the sacred and the secular. Indeed ecology can be seen as an expression of an integrated spirituality. There is a further point to be made. There is more and more to be known about our world. Scientists and scholars will continue to discover secrets of this universe still hidden from us. How important to remember that all discovery and research is an exploration of the mind of God. Truth is in God first before being known by us. Future knowledge and the future itself has to be welcomed and anticipated without foreboding as revelation and realisation of God in our world.

All searching for God on our part is our personal response to his searching for us. I began with the experience of a great English mystic; Julian of Norwich understood that our whole existence is proof of God's unceasing love for us. It is an understanding rooted deeply in the Gospels. St Luke's Gospel, for instance, in chapter 15 unfolds for us in a series of unforgettable images our Lord's assurance that God, in his love, searches tirelessly for what has gone astray and seems, with a kind of divine perversity, to long even more tenderly for the wayward than for those who never leave his side. Jesus tells us of the shepherd who leaves the ninety-nine sheep in the wilderness to go in search of the one that has strayed. And then rejoices at finding 'my sheep which was lost'. He tells also of the woman with ten silver coins who loses one and cannot rest until it is found. She calls her friends and neighbours to rejoice with her 'for I have found the coin which I had lost'. And the sequence of parables reaches its climax with the story of the prodigal son who abandoned his father's house in search of fame and fortune, and was reduced to poverty and despair. On his return he was met by his father who had never ceased to await his coming and who greeted him with overwhelming warmth and welcome. The unmistakable conclusion is that we are cherished by God our Father who simply cannot cease to love us. We cannot command or earn his love. We have no need to. He created us in love; he made us in the image of himself, in the Word through whom all things were made. He will not, cannot, let us go. The divine love which made all things, keeps them in being, brings them to their goal which is also their beginning.

This is a fundamental assurance which is at the heart of all spiritual life, all vital communion with God. The awareness of being loved, of being called into life, is not a sentimental feeling, a variable in our experience. It goes deeper than words, must endure amid storms, darkness, distractions and dereliction.

In our emptiness and sense of failure we can and must turn always to the fulfilment of God's covenant with humanity. The Word became flesh and dwelt among us. It is in Christ that the human and the divine meet. God emptied himself and became as we are in all that is not sin. Through the incarnation the taking by God of our human nature and his involvement in our human history redeems all that is human, gives it a glory that no subsequent sin and rebellion can ever ultimately deface or destroy. Our human world, our humanity is re-fashioned in Christ and is assured of an everlasting destiny. To come to him in faith, to die with him in order to live, opens up for us a new creation, new heavens and a new earth, in which we see God in Christ and discern the face of God. 'Have I been with you so long,' says Christ, 'and yet you do not know me, Philip? He who has seen me has seen the Father; how can you say, "Show us the Father"? Do you not believe that I am in the Father and the Father is in me?' (John 14:9–10). To imagine that we still cannot 'put a face' to God, that we are still 'in the dark' about the reality of divine love and compassion, is to ignore perhaps the blindingly obvious and fail to linger long enough on the features and the personality of Jesus Christ. Here surely we can learn to enter into 'conversation' with God. The words of our Lord, his every action are recorded in time but are 'outside' time, as relevant and grace-filled for us today as for any other generation. And our meditation will lead us gently but insistently from the concrete circumstances and life of Christ in history to his abiding presence among us not only in the sacraments but in that body of Christ which is the Church. We learn there to love the cosmic Christ, the eternal Word.

The consequences of the incarnation are vital for us; throughout the liturgical year we have opportunities to deepen our understanding of what our Lord did to save us from our sinfulness and restore us to intimacy with the Father. I wish here only to make two points, both familiar to you, but none the less very profound. First, the very fact of the incarnation means that all that is human has been touched by the divine, except, of course, for sin. The ancient Christian writers pointed out that since our Lord stood in the Jordan to be baptised, all water has therefore been sanctified. Secondly, our Lord's public ministry lasted about three to three and a half years. Thirty years of his life was spent leading the ordinary life of a person of his day in Nazareth. Those years were precious in the eyes of his Father and so were all the activities of his Son, each one of value – human acts done by one who was God. Thus all our actions, and especially in virtue of our baptism, have a special value in the eyes of God. The Father sees in you and me the image or reflection of his Son, and finds what we do precious in his sight.

It is important to remember the value of what we do each day. If we are aware of this then we escape from the trap of seeing some activities as spiritually worthwhile (such as attendance in church or prayer), and others as entirely secular with no relationship to God, save to avoid displeasing him by sin. To live in the light of that dichotomy is to have failed to appreciate one of the most important consequences of the incarnation.

It would be wrong to give the impression that our striving to know and love God and God's search for us happens in isolation from the people and purely in the higher reaches of one's being. We are destined for God as whole beings, body and soul. Christ's mission to the world healed both body and soul. And we are baptised into a single body, made one *in* Christ as well as one *with* Christ. Our spiritual life is therefore always personal but never individualistic. It remains very personal because the spiritual life is concerned with our union with God which must always be an embrace of love between two persons. It is never individualistic since its primary focus must always be God not me, and since God loves me – and all that he made – in Christ, the Word. The love God has for me is shared by others. God loves them, relates to them, embraces them as he does me.

But there is more than this. By baptism we die to our self-centred, sinful isolation and are plunged into the very heart of God's life and love. Our identification with Christ, our incorporation into him, is complete. God recreates us as his sons and daughters, members of the body of his beloved Son. The Holy Spirit indwells in us as living temples. We know and are known in the Son. We love and are loved in the Holy Spirit. Already here and now we begin to share eternal life. Sharing in these divine realities fashions bonds between the baptised which are closer and stronger than any human ties of blood or race; we are one people of God, his sons and daughters, one body of Christ, one temple in which dwells the Holy Spirit.

Thus we cannot say that we love God if we do not love all those identified with the Son of God: those in whom the life of God already shines, as well as those who are made in the Word but have not yet consciously adhered to him. St John tells us that 'if God so loved us, we also ought to love one another. No man has ever seen God; if we love one another, God abides in us and his love is perfected in us' (1 John 4:11–12). Jesus Christ himself warned us that if we ignore any of the basic needs of others, then we are guilty of neglecting him, we fail to be channels of the Father's love (Matt. 25). If we do not listen to others, recognising their relationship with God, then we close our ears to the Holy Spirit who speaks through them.

The task ahead of us in renewing the Church in our day is perhaps no more than letting the life and love of God have fuller play in our individual lives and in the mission and ministry of the Christian community.

Practical programmes for developing the spiritual life are best drawn up to suit individual and local circumstances. I have tried to indicate some general principles behind such development and these in turn will suggest some requirements for any particular programme. Since people will become holy in the circumstances in which they find themselves and through discovering God in the people, places and things they encounter daily, the centres for spiritual development should be where people are, namely in the parishes and local communities. It is here that priests, religious and laity working together need to fashion ways of developing their spiritual awareness, becoming open to the Word of God and allowing themselves to be touched and shaped by the power and presence of God in their lives. Guides for this spiritual pilgrimage will be needed so we should make provision for the training of men and women as spiritual directors and making them more generally available at parish level. At the same time, to ensure that all spiritual formation is rooted in the reality of daily life, we could perhaps try to develop parish centres devoted to the study and application of the teaching of the Council decree on the mission and role of the Church in the modern world to local conditions and to the integration of prayer and life. It is almost certainly true that the parish community itself is too large for the kind of spiritual development which is necessary. Small groups will have to be created to study the word of God, to pray together, to explore the things of God through meditation and action. These groups will not be inward-looking but could become the living heart of the parish, giving vitality and depth to the parish Sunday Eucharist and engaging in the caring, healing and reconciling ministry of the Church in the locality. Individuals should be encouraged to search for God in all the circumstances of their daily lives. As I have already said, they cannot for the most part enjoy in their crowded lives the space and silence which priests and religious so take for granted. They have to learn to cultivate the art of withdrawal in the midst of bustle and activity. They can create – albeit with difficulty – an inner sanctuary where they commune with God. They seize every opportunity for conscious awareness of his presence but in all things and at all times they realise that they are in the midst of God's revealing of himself and are part of his outpoured life and love. At the heart of this renewal is a deeper appreciation of the Eucharist, of the celebration of Mass. Christ told us, in words we repeat whenever we offer the supreme sacrifice of the Mass, 'Do this in memory of me.' We recall his death, his resurrection and his ascension into heaven, not in a merely commemorative sense, but in a way which makes present and real the saving mystery of Christ of which we are now intimately and wholly a part. The Eucharist is source and summit of all our living and loving as body of Christ. The spiritual life is our conscious share in that mystery.

I began with Julian of Norwich, let her have the final word:

So it was that I learned that love was Our Lord's meaning. And I saw for certain, both here and elsewhere, that before ever he made us, God loved us; and that his love has never slackened, nor ever shall. In this love all his works have been done, and in this love he has made everything serve us; and in this love our life is everlasting. Our beginning was

when we were made, but the love in which he made us
never had beginning. In it we have our beginning.

All this we shall see in God for ever. May Jesus grant this.
Amen.

8

The Church as Educator

We are distinctively human because we are able to know and to love. Jewish and Christian believers alike have concluded that we are made in the image and likeness of God since through our powers of intellect and will we are enabled to share his life and love. Experience teaches us that both faculties are interdependent since we cannot love without knowledge nor truly know unless we love. This enables us to relate to all that is. Relationships give shape, meaning and purpose to our lives. Yet in forming relationships knowledge comes first and determines what it is we love. That is why it is essential to our very humanity that we should be free to develop to the utmost our capacity to reason, learn and comprehend in order that we may love and relate. In so doing we act in a way which is both human and divine. This, in essence, is the explanation of the Church's remarkable commitment to, and deep concern for, everything that pertains to education and the pursuit of truth. We are here at the heart of our own humanity and at the same time in the sphere of true religion.

Enemies of the Christian faith have recognised this clearly. In the long and bitter struggle with religion throughout this century, Communist regimes have sometimes tolerated public worship but have usually suppressed Church schools and centres of learning, prohibited public religious instruction and denied the churches access to the means of mass communication. The school and the lecture-hall are seen as significant in the battle for minds and hearts and in laying foundations for community and a common purpose. Social reformers of every kind are anxious to exert influence on the educational system and thus to pave the way for radical change. The Church, by contrast, does not see education simply as a means to an end but as an integral part of her mission to evangelise, reconcile and renew. As such it is obviously a matter of immense importance.

Catholic schools are now spread throughout the world. They are responsible for the education of millions of pupils. Official statistics reveal that on December 31st, 1985 there were 154,126 Catholic schools with 38,243,304 students. This immense enterprise, involving perhaps some 4 per cent of young people throughout the world, should come as no surprise to those who know anything of the history of the Catholic Church.

Throughout the Dark Ages in Europe it was largely through the work of the Church that the flame of classical learning was not entirely extinguished. In these islands the Catholic Church established the first schools and universities. And to this day the churches have continued to make a major contribution to education nationally. They have worked alongside the state in the provision and development of the nation's schools. The partnership in Britain of statutory and voluntary bodies in this endeavour, the dual system, is a remarkable achievement and one that should be jealously safeguarded. Once damaged it cannot easily be repaired.

Education shapes the life of every individual. Schools are a major means whereby the knowledge and achievements of previous generations are communicated and become the foundation of future progress. They help to transmit and develop values and a generation's faith and vision. When an educational system appears to be in difficulties there is good reason for public anxiety. When it breaks down a whole society is threatened.

Few would dispute that some reform is necessary in schools as they struggle to educate pupils to live in a confusing and changing world. There is for many young people, not only in our own country, a sense that stability and security are no more, that signposts and standards have been swept away and that violence, alcohol, drugs and promiscuous sex have to be employed in a desperate attempt to fill the void at the heart of so much modern life. For some a sense of mystery and transcendence has been lost; only material and financial rewards are felt to be worthwhile. There is in many quarters a curious collective amnesia, a loss of any sense of history, and a cynicism about the future which leads to an emphasis on short-term objectives and immediate quantifiable results. All of this affects the intellectual climate of society and inevitably influences attitudes towards education.

The shortcomings of our national educational system have been widely publicised but while there is a measure of agreement about them there is still no consensus on how to put them right, no agreed theoretical basis for reform. It has seemed to many of us in the churches and elsewhere that the package of proposals included in the Education Reform Act was put together initially with undue haste and after inadequate consultation. Sometimes it seemed that political rather than educational considerations predominated. The Roman Catholic bishops' conference of England and Wales drew attention to three major anxieties about the bill as it passed through Parliament. They concerned the place of religious education in the curriculum, admission policies in relation to voluntary schools and the effect on the Catholic school system in particular of the proposals about grant-aided status. Some, but not all, of our anxieties were met but I suspect there has not been a true meeting of minds.

In the course of the lengthy controversy about the proposed legislation, it became increasingly clear to me that many people, including some Catholics, were unclear about the role of the Church in education and the distinctive character of Catholic schools. Without renewed understanding and increased support on all sides, the unique Catholic contribution to education will inevitably suffer. There is need for an informed and vigorous debate about our Catholic schools and what they offer to the Catholic community and society in general at a time of rapid and profound change. The voice of the Church should also be heard in the continuing exchanges about the future of education in our country. We have a coherent philosophy and a vision of education that we believe to be of universal significance. To understand the positive aspects of the Church's present position it will be necessary to focus more sharply on the arguments about the nature of religious education and about the complex partnership of trustees, foundation governors and parents. This latter reveals the Church's attitude towards its community responsibilities and stewardship.

God is the heart of religious education and the purpose of all education. Many might understand this in a narrow and restrictive sense. What is so frequently lost sight of today is, however, the overwhelming truth I have attempted to present in this book, that 'God is in everything and everything is in God'. In education as in all life we need to develop an ever deeper understanding of Christian teaching about the Triune God, Father, Son and Holy Spirit, and of the Judaeo-Christian concept of creation. Here, I would suggest, is the crux of the matter. Belief about the nature of God is not abstract and irrelevant. It shapes all our perceptions of reality and all our responses. At the same time a vivid and all-embracing awareness of creation as a single and continuing expression of God's overwhelming goodness and love must, of necessity, affect all knowledge and all values. In one sense, religious education is not a subject at all but a constantly developing way of learning how to look at the world and ourselves and the relationship of all creation to the creator God. It embraces and enlivens every other subject in a school's curriculum. It is, as the present Holy Father said to the bishops of the Westminster province in March 1988, 'the core of the core curriculum'.

Knowledge, a trained mind and different skills are essential to fit a young person for a career. But there is more – or at any rate should be. The Pope in the speech quoted above went on to say: 'If religion is neglected or set aside in the educational process that forms a nation's heart and soul, then a morality worthy of man will not survive, justice and peace will not endure.' Inculcating a sense of the ultimate purpose of life and moral norms to determine behaviour is, surely, an equally important part of the educational process.

Preparing for a career is not all. The pursuit and possession of truth for its own sake are values in themselves. Not all that is studied in school or university must needs be at the service of some utilitarian purpose. Just to know and to delight in knowledge is part of the working of the human mind.

This is especially so when it is realised how all discovery and research are an exploration into the mind of God, and knowledge a sharing in it. It is too when a person discovers that contemplation of God through that which falls within our experience can be one of the most satisfying of all intellectual pursuits. Thus in all that is true, good or beautiful the mind glimpses how they can each reflect in a marvellous manner the reality which we call God. This is to know him in his creation, as the artist leaves something of himself in his work of art. This, surely, is what St Paul had in mind when he wrote: 'For what can be known about God is plain to them, because God has shown it to them. Ever since the creation of the world his invisible nature, namely, his eternal power and deity, has been clearly perceived in the things that have been made' (Rom. 1:19–20).

What is immediately obvious is that the imparting of such a total vision of life cannot be left solely to the efforts of any school however effective and dedicated. It is a process which necessarily involves the family and the local community of faith, the parish. Each plays an indispensable role in a partnership that calls urgently for immediate development.

The sad decline in family life has undoubtedly often left its mark on children. The breakdown of so many marriages deprives them of stability and the constant affection and encouragement necessary for their spiritual, moral and psychological growth. The Second Vatican Council clearly recognised the importance of the family in a child's education.

The role of parents in education is of such importance that it is almost impossible to provide an adequate substitute . . . The family is therefore the principal school of the social virtues which are necessary to every society. It is therefore above all in the Christian family, inspired by the grace and the responsibility of the sacrament of matrimony, that children should be taught to know and worship God and to love their neighbour, in accordance with the faith which they have received in earliest infancy in the sacrament of baptism. In it, also, they will have their first experience of a well-balanced human society and of the Church. Finally it is through the family that they are gradually initiated into association with their fellow men in civil life and as members of the people of God. (Declaration on Catholic Education, N.3)

When the foundations are shaky or non-existent, then parish and school have little or nothing on which to build.

The role of the parish in the religious growth of the child and young adult is sometimes not given sufficient care and attention. In our islands the custom of bringing even infants to Sunday Mass with the rest of the family remains thankfully strong. It is important, despite all the obvious difficulties, to welcome the whole family to the weekly celebration which is the source and summit of the life of the people of God. It is also important that the young be encouraged to grow in their understanding, appreciation and sharing in the Mass. An increasing number of parishes now provide for the young their own liturgy of the Word so that the reading and reflection in the scriptures is better suited to their stage of development. Provided this can be done with appropriate skill and children can then rejoin their families for the rest of the Mass, there is every possibility of their growing in love for the liturgy.

Considerable thought needs to be given to the initiation of the young into the life of the people of God in the parish. It is not a matter of simply providing entertainment and sporting facilities for them – important though these often are – but of gradually introducing them into that fellowship of service which is Christian love in action. Each community needs to think through how best to effect this. In society today it can never be taken for granted that children will follow in their parents' footsteps. There is no social pressure to reinforce parental ideals and religious faith. Like it or not, this is an age of choice and so we need all our experience, conviction and imaginative empathy to help the young to choose wisely and well.

The role of the church school in partnership with family and parish is presently the subject of much discussion and careful reflection. It is becoming, I am convinced, increasingly clear that the Catholic school is even more necessary today at a time of much social and moral fragmentation. The Declaration on Catholic Education, already quoted, has this to say:

> The Catholic school pursues cultural goals and the natural development of youth to the same degree as any other school. What makes the Catholic school distinctive is its attempt to generate a community climate in the school that is permeated by the Gospel spirit of freedom and love. It tries to guide the adolescents in such a way that personality development goes hand in hand with the development of the 'new creature' that each one has become through baptism. It tries to relate all of human culture to the good news of salvation so that the light of faith will illumine everything that the students will gradually come to learn about the world, about life and about the human person. (N.8)

As recent guidelines produced by the Congregation for Catholic Education point out, the distinctive character of the Catholic school is to be found in its educational climate, the personal development of each student, the relationship between culture and the Gospel and the illumination of all knowledge with the light of faith.

It has become clear, I think, that Catholic schools, whatever their present performance, are being urged to rise to new heights. They should embody and develop their own ethos that can be described perhaps as a religious humanism. Staff and pupils in a sense depend upon each other to translate the ideal into reality. There should be room in the school for the enjoyment of every kind of activity – academic, artistic, technical, manual and sporting – and the encouragement of every kind of talent. The common denominators should be a thirst for excellence in whatever is attempted and a sheer delight in the activity for its own sake. As I have already indicated, knowledge has significance and value irrespective of its usefulness. Education can never be simply the acquiring of job-skills but must embrace the growth of the whole person.

Every pupil should be encouraged 'to stand and stare', to relish beauty for its own sake. In truth and beauty we can all catch a glimpse of the divine. We have to make these points again and again.

It is surely clear that a task of such magnitude can be carried out only by a school community whose staff and pupils share a life of faith and Christian love. In the plural society in which we live such unity and solidarity are rare; we cannot expect them to be the ethos of an avowedly secular school. Yet pluralism which requires mutual respect and freedom in society cannot by definition rule out the right and responsibility of a Church to provide for its young people the opportunity to grow in an integrated way in both knowledge and faith. Harmony, balance, a clear sense of meaning and purpose are the distinguishing marks of a good Catholic education. They are our best contribution to the plural society.

It is obvious that I am proposing an ideal which few, if any of us, would claim to have adequately translated into practice. To have any hope of our doing so the Church itself must collectively ensure that the best possible environment is created. We owe to our teaching staffs, past and present, an incalculable debt of gratitude. Today it is harder than ever to maintain a steady flow of teachers who share our educational vision and are willing to uphold its Christian values. Without them our schools will lose their direction and sense of purpose. There is urgent need to restore to the teaching profession the respect and the rewards to which it is plainly entitled. The Catholic community, too, should renew its efforts to encourage young students to enter the profession. Good teachers make good schools. Without them the future is bleak indeed.

The growth of the school as a community of faith and love depends also, of course, on its pupils. There has to be a basic sympathy among the young with the ethos and values of their school. It would prove a disastrous penalty for success if a popular school were to be compelled to admit those who do not fundamentally share its view of the world. The instinct of Catholic priests and teachers is to open the doors of the school to all baptised Catholics no matter what the faith commitment of their parents. This certainly provides pupils with an opportunity to experience something of the Catholic faith in action. Is there, however, evidence of lasting benefit to the children of the lapsed from their attendance at a Catholic school? A non-practising pupil can react negatively to the school's religious ethos. And there is undoubtedly the risk of reducing dangerously the total level of religious commitment in the school if too many pupils are indifferent to their faith. Similarly it would be wrong to alter the atmosphere of the school by too liberal an open-door policy for those of other churches and other faiths. Christian ecumenical schools have broken new ground in some places and may well be a significant indication of a way forward. The haphazard admission, however, of non-Catholics and those of other faiths creates obvious problems and the situation will have to be examined carefully to ensure the best way forward. There are no easy answers to the questions posed by these dilemmas, but the search for answers is becoming increasingly urgent.

In general the Church must uphold the principle that the voluntary church school is a recognisable community of faith. It should commend itself immediately by its attitudes and its approach to the whole process of education.

The Catholic school community should be making explicit but non-verbal statements about itself from the moment one enters its gates. If it is based on a true awareness of God, there should be an almost tangible atmosphere of freedom, welcome and warmth. Care, concern and respect for people as children of God should be demonstrated in the attitudes of staff to pupils and of pupils to each other. Individuals will be valued for themselves irrespective of ability and achievement. There will be a noticeable sense of unity and family which will affect the way that discipline is exercised without brutality or indifference. A remarkable feature of so many of our Catholic schools is that young people will devote themselves generously and selflessly to those who suffer from any kind of distress. They will respond with enthusiasm to the needs of the old and the handicapped in their area. They will undertake projects to raise money for the starving and destitute in the Third World. Teachers, sharing this concern, can help the young to realise that their instincts of compassion are not a passing enthusiasm but an expression of their basic humanity and solidarity with all the human family. On a more domestic level concern for others and for the environment should be evident in the care taken of the natural surroundings of the school and of the building itself. There should be beauty, orderliness and an absence of vandalism. Religious symbols should be well-chosen and their influence pervasive. Physical surroundings can so often indicate a state of mind or an attitude of belief.

Throughout the Catholic school there should be evident a realisation that education has to develop the whole person. The classroom itself is only part of it. If any pupil leaves the school feeling altogether diminished by failure, the school itself has failed perhaps by an over-emphasis on some one aspect of education. The school itself should provide positive and creative experiences for all its pupils, academically gifted or not, so that each and every one learns to grow at different levels, psychological, social, artistic, physical and emotional. Success is never to be measured solely by examination results or job-skills gained. A school has ultimately to be judged on the kind of people it has helped to develop and on how they are being equipped for life here and in the hereafter. Much depends on the quality of relationships that exist in a school community. These ultimately are decisive both for learning at every level and for growing in faith and commitment. It is important to realise that all education involves not just learning the truth but living it as well. And any attempt to do this creates tangible changes in behaviour and in the environment we create around ourselves.

I have said little explicitly so far about the content of the Catholic school's curriculum. There has been much discussion on the place of religious education among the essential subjects to be taught in every school. Religious studies, as part of our young people's total education, can be and should be intellectually stimulating and have a content and depth which require rigorous planning and detailed attention to methodology and evaluation. They are not woolly and undemanding and are not to be replaced by, or compared with, the often inadequate excursions into comparative religion favoured by many today. They draw into a coherent whole all that is contained in the curriculum.

In the past there was a danger that pupils might know answers to questions, without any deep religious experience. Today there may be a danger of seeking and analysing religious experience without knowing that which should guide and enrich it. It would be quite wrong to conclude that religious education should be largely an exercise in self-discovery and subjectivity. That has its place but there is much more. The Christian religion is based upon divine revelation which comes from without and is embraced by faith. Christian believers need to be introduced to all the richness of scripture and tradition. There is objective truth to be studied. Two millennia of Church teaching and an incomparable wealth of theology, moral principle and spiritual insight await the serious enquirer. Catholic education is impoverished if it neglects this heritage and our young people are thereby deprived of their intellectual and religious birthright.

A recent paper entitled 'Evaluating the distinctive nature of a Catholic school' by a working party of the bishops' conference summed it up thus:

The Church sees education as part of its mission to proclaim God as Creator, Christ the Redeemer and the Holy Spirit as Indwelling Inspirer of all that is good in human living. The Church believes that the created order speaks of God, that human relationships are redeemed by Christ's saving death and resurrection, and that real human advancement and achievement testify to the Holy Spirit at work in humanity enabling everyone to grow and develop. God is at work in his world and can be discovered in our daily living, drawing us to himself in love, inviting us to grow in a relationship with him as the most perfect fulfilment of our lives. This means that, despite our sinfulness or shortcomings, every person's life is charged with God's presence and every human experience presents us with the opportunity to deepen our knowledge and love of Him. Therefore, the process of education, teaching and learning, is a holy act and, since the world in which we live is God's, all teaching and learning is somehow related to Him. Everything connected with human living, and the means by which we understand and come to terms with it, is part of the process of God's self-revelation to humanity, whether those engaged in it are conscious of it or not.

In a Catholic school there should be a single vision embracing religion and life, a unity which does no violence to the academic disciplines and rightful autonomy of each subject in the curriculum.

Distinctive to a Catholic school should be its attitude as a community to prayer and worship, not as an imposed obligation but as a spontaneous response to life and to learning. The school encourages and leads pupils in an organised exploration of God's creation by means of the whole curriculum and so brings them increasingly into a conscious encounter with the Creator. Pupils and staff should find ways of articulating and making their own a response to God both in private prayer and in public worship. The supreme prayer of the people of god is the Eucharist or Thanksgiving. We are thus constantly reminded that we are literally nothing without God but are created and sustained by his life and love given us as free gift. The Christian community of the school, like the people of God in every circumstance, has a duty to give heartfelt thanks and glory to God. The worship of the school takes many forms. Assemblies, either of the whole school or sections of it, have to be rescued from formalism and irrelevance. They should be prepared with care and sensitivity to ensure that they are appropriate to the age-range and levels of development among the pupils. There is obviously more scope and potential for real prayer in the classroom setting. Children often are not taught to pray at home or not encouraged to do so. If they are to learn to pray then, realistically, the school is the only place they are likely to be taught. The range of possibilities is great and can provide a foundation for the regular celebration of the liturgy in schools. Here, as in so many other ways, there should be much closer partnership between home, parish and school. Perhaps the school chaplain is the key to this development.

Emphasis on religious education and spiritual formation should not be taken as any indication of indifference on the part of the Church towards other parts of the curriculum or other school activities. Nor should the ideal Catholic school be seen as in any sense elitist and divisive. The purpose of the Catholic school is not to perpetuate the ghetto or to alienate or set apart young Catholics from their peers. There is a comprehensiveness and a sense of genuine humanity in the best Catholic tradition that should motivate staff and pupils to look outward, to be involved with others, to live lives of true compassion. The case for the Catholic school is that it develops a personal Christian faith, an attachment to Christian values and a constructive and responsible attitude towards life. It gives a young Catholic also a genuine experience of community which helps his or her growth in the people of God.

The school community, after all, has no meaning except in relation to the Church, the universal community of faith. It is impossible to make sense of a church school in isolation. Each particular church, each diocese, in the name of all its members and their families, has laboured mightily over many generations to provide for all the children of that community the possibility of a Catholic education. The bishop as leader of that community and in its name holds most of the Catholic schools in trust, apart from some owned and operated usually by religious orders. It is a planned provision which matches local needs and, because it is a community service, it has the long-term interests of that community at heart. It is the fruit of positive partnership between pastors and people. The faith of the community shaped the voluntary school system; the community made great financial sacrifices to achieve it; many generations have contributed to its growth. The Catholic community looks to its bishop to act as trustee for its schools, not as autocrat but as spiritual father and as symbolising in his office and person all that they hold precious in their fellowship of faith. The bishop in all he does is the focus of unity in the community. He is charged by his office to consider the welfare of all his flock and to act accordingly. In his role as trustee of diocesan schools he is in duty bound to secure the best interests of each school and also to ensure that the whole community is well served by the provision of appropriate schools in any area. In this he will normally have particular regard for those who are otherwise disadvantaged.

The role of the bishop as trustee and of the foundation

governors he appoints to the governing body of each school has become a matter of great importance for the future of our voluntary school system and for the contribution it can make to national education. Between them, trustee and governors guarantee its independence and effectiveness. Not everyone appreciates this. Those charged with maintaining the voluntary system need to look beyond the legal to wider moral responsibilities.

The distinctive character of the Catholic school, so essential for Church and society, is enshrined in a trust deed. The trustee is responsible for implementing the trust deed and foundation governors are entrusted with the carrying out of this responsibility in the case of individual schools. Diocesan trust deeds provide 'for property to be held on trusts of advancing the Roman Catholic religion in the diocese by such means as the Ordinary (Bishop) may think it fit and proper'. Overall planning of Catholic education within the diocese is part of that responsibility. The foundation governors of individual schools can reasonably be expected to take this into account. The Cardinal Prefect of the Congregation for Catholic Education recently wrote to me from the Vatican clarifying from a Catholic point of view an important principle:

> Individual Catholics who are 'governors' of Catholic schools in the 'dual system' must not only know and fulfil their statutory obligations but must also know their ecclesial rights and obligations. In other words they are to respond to the State's and the Church's legitimate expectations of them in such a way as to fulfil their responsibilities both as citizens and as Catholics. The management of one Catholic school should be conducted with due regard for the needs of other Catholic schools and for the interests of Catholic education in general as determined by the bishop of the diocese. (Cardinal Baum, October 16th, 1987)

These complex and rather remote matters of law and administration are, however, highly relevant to the whole concept of Catholic education and to the planning and administration of our schools. If the Catholic school system is to be supported and developed in future it is essential to avoid fragmentation and the pursuit of sectional interests at the expense of the wider needs of the community. Options may be legally available, but can be positively harmful if they are taken up without prior consultation and the consent of the community expressed through the trustee. This involves the risk of inflicting serious and perhaps lasting damage on the Catholic community as a whole with consequent harm to society.

The system of Church schools should be clearly at the service of the wider community. Undoubtedly others who are not themselves Catholic wish to place their children in our schools for a variety of reasons. They appreciate the many good characteristics of our schools and want their children to benefit from these even if they do not subscribe completely to the beliefs on which the school is based. Sometimes their appreciation of our schools outstrips that of our own Catholic parents. But I would suggest there is a more general and direct contribution which our schools make to the community.

The Catholic schools are, in fact, apart from monasteries, convents and religious houses, almost the only example of Catholic communities in daily existence and operation. Parishes function fully only in the celebration of the liturgy when the community is united in worship. Their pastoral and social life is not comprehensive. The school on the other hand brings together large assemblies daily, is dedicated to the Christian ideal and strives to live by it. A school should be seen not only as communicating to the young an understanding of the world but as a living embodiment of a vision and a way of life and as a witness to society. It practises what it preaches about the individual dignity and worth of each person; it endeavours to release each one's full potential. And it brings into unity every aspect of life: there is no gap between religion and life; all truths are seen as revealing the unity of creation and its oneness with God; past, present and future are brought into the focus of faith and are recognised as God's continuing act of creation. Far from assimilating Church schools into the national system it would seem essential to the well-being of the nation that they be maintained and strengthened in their cherished independence. They are rooted in our past; they provide a hope for the future of today's world.

9

To Proclaim the Good News

In January 1986 Pope John Paul sent a remarkable letter to all
the presidents of bishops' conferences throughout Europe.
In March 1987, in Frankfurt, they gathered to discuss their
joint response to the Holy Father and to consider what shared
initiatives might give effect to his proposals. They face a
daunting and complex task because the Holy Father is urging
them and the churches they lead to undertake new efforts to
evangelise, or rather re-evangelise, the whole continent of
Europe.

Surprisingly there was not a great deal of publicity when the
Pope's letter was originally published. Yet in fact it de-
molished quite a few of the myths current about the Pope and
the policies of the Holy See. The letter itself, for instance, was
addressed to the presidents of national conferences throughout Europe, thereby witnessing to the importance of the
conferences and their role in the life and mission of the
Church. It also contained a powerful plea for the strengthening of the Council of European bishops' conferences, since
action at continental level is needed to tackle common problems. The approach, too, must be specifically European; it
has to be adapted to the culture and traditions of the continent. In all these ways the Holy Father can be seen as
implicitly accepting important principles of inculturation and
subsidiarity as well as embracing the spirit of collegiality.

The Pope's letter highlights the significance of Europe and

its changing role in the world and the Church. There can be no doubt of the importance of our continent in the history of the world, nor of the European contribution to the universal Church. We have been responsible for great blessings and for many disasters; our continent has exported both good things and bad.

From Europe Christian missionaries have taken the Christian Gospel to the world, but at the same time they perpetuated the religious divisions which had their origin here. Political rivalries and conflicts have also spread abroad. India, North America and Africa, for example, suffered from the colonial ambitions of European countries in competition with each other. In this century two world wars were caused in the first instance by European struggles. The present East/West tension, originating in Europe, still has the whole world in its grip after four decades. Our continent has been a cockpit of conflict; despite present disarmament initiatives it remains the possible setting for a nuclear Armageddon that could bring human history to a ghastly and tragic conclusion.

There can be little doubt that the political and religious scene is changing. The balance of power and influence is shifting slowly but perceptibly. No longer is Europe the undisputed centre of the political world, just as the European churches are no longer decisive in the affairs of the universal Church. It was, for instance, noticeable at the Extraordinary Synod of 1985 when each conference of bishops was represented by its president, that over 60 per cent of those present came from Third World countries. In less than a lifetime, from the time when bishops from the young churches were first appointed and ordained, the Church worldwide has ceased to be predominantly European in culture and numbers and has become, for the first time in history, Catholic not only in name but in reality.

Yet Europe still has much to offer both the world and the Church; not only the lessons of its history but its hard-won values, technological expertise, academic standards and its long experience of social and political institutions are of particular significance. There is, too, the witness of a spiritual and human search by Europe for healing and new life. After the ravages of two wars and centuries of religious conflict, may we dare to hope that Europe at last seems set on discovering a better way?

The second half of this century has been marked by a search for greater political unity and cooperation. The European Community and the Council of Europe are tangible, if limited, achievements. Similarly the Christian churches have been engaged in discussions and joint action in attempts to overcome the dissensions which have split Church unity in Europe since the initial division between East and West a thousand years ago.

In the depths of European consciousness today, it is possible to discern a profound change and the dawning of a realisation that we are entering a new phase of history. The age of Enlightenment has evidently run its course. This idea was explored by Dr Lesslie Newbigin in a paper produced for the British Council of Churches entitled 'Beyond 1984'. He maintains that beyond all doubt we have seen the limitations of human reason as a means for exploring religious truth and for establishing an alternative value-system to the revealed truth of Christianity. At the same time we have been brought to the brink of nuclear destruction after two devastating world wars and have seen that technological mastery is no substitute for spiritual and moral maturity. We have now glimpsed what our future might become. So we do need to find a new and better way forward. This must involve every level of society. The political will has to be found to adopt solutions with vigour and determination. The Church plays its part in this process. It can never work alone or in isolation from all those other institutions and individuals whose contribution to the healing and rebuilding of society is so crucial. The Church has to take seriously and pursue with faith and determination that renewal whose essential elements were agreed at the Second Vatican Council. It must also, as the Pope so insistently reminds us, find new and effective ways of evangelising today's world.

Renewal and re-evangelisation are therefore essential if the Church is to undertake effectively her mission in the world. These two are inextricably linked – there can be no effective evangelisation without an authentic renewal, by which I mean that change of heart of which the Gospel speaks so insistently.

Renewal leads inevitably to sharing the Gospel message with others. Structural changes of themselves do not effect conversion and renewal. To discover how spiritual renewal is brought about is the major need of our time and one to which I refer elsewhere in this book. The fact that an increasing number are aware of this is, perhaps, a small beginning.

The process of renewal in spirituality, liturgy and theology has already begun. Re-evangelisation, on the other hand, is a task only now becoming evident. Although the needs of the modern world were deeply felt in the 1960s, it is only now becoming obvious how depleted is the spiritual and religious heritage of the western world and how urgently needed is a radical evangelisation of our society. We are, as Catholics, approaching this undertaking somewhat hesitantly. We have grown accustomed in Europe to being pastors and not missionaries. We can be excused for feeling daunted at the size and complexity of what is needed. We require accurate analysis of the contemporary situation. We need a more consistent and energetic response if our generation is to hear the Gospel of Jesus Christ. The letter of Pope John Paul to the presidents of the bishops' conferences of Europe leaves us in no doubt as to the urgency and importance of this task. He says:

> The profound and complex cultural, political, ethical and spiritual transformations that have given a new face to the fabric of European society must be matched by a new quality of evangelisation such as will succeed in setting before modern man the ageless message of salvation in convincing terms. Europe needs to be given a soul and a new self-awareness. (N.6)

The Extraordinary Synod which took place in Rome in November 1985 and the 1987 Synod on the Laity together form a certain unity and help us to measure how successfully the Council has been implemented. It is helpful to reflect a little on the experience so far of the Synod of Bishops. It is in its present form a relatively new structure in the Church. Its procedure and conventions are subject to change and development. Its relationship to other bodies is still evolving. It helps to express, at present imperfectly, that sense of collegial responsibility on the part of the world's bishops for the welfare of the whole Church.

The Synod of Bishops is, as we know, only consultative in character and provides a means of communicating to the Supreme Pastor the concerns and hopes of particular churches throughout the world. It provides us with helpful – if general – guidance for pastoral practice. At local level it gives us opportunity to focus on particular areas of concern, consult about present conditions, contribute to international discussions and later reflect on the teaching which emerges from the deliberations. Each synod should be a further step along the road of renewal; it is up to particular churches how far progress is made along that road. We can, as a whole people of God, thus become slowly more aware of what it means to be Church in our world.

The Synod on the Role of the Laity could in no sense be regarded as a decisive moment in the life of the Church; it is best seen as another stage on a journey of self-understanding and renewal. This is the context within which we should be looking at the role and mission of the laity. We need to see how the vision of the Council is being translated into reality.

It will be very easy to feel disappointment, since the vocation of the laity, described by the Council, is to 'play their part in that mission entrusted to the whole people of God, play it both inside the Church and out in the world; play it as priests, prophets and kings, because they too have been made sharers of the priestly, prophetic and royal work of Christ' (Decree on the Laity, N.2). These words remind us that we must not fall into a rather tempting trap. Because the 1987 Synod focused on the pastoral needs of the laity, it does not mean that we should consider the laity in isolation. The laity, clergy and religious together make up the one people of God; they share the same mission; they carry out that mission in different ways and in different settings, but it would be a mistake to insist too rigidly on a distinction of roles. The ministries of clergy and laity are different but they are complementary; they reinforce and support each other; it is unhelpful to assign to the clergy an exclusively 'churchy' role and to the laity exclusively a secular one. Laity have a role within the life of the Church as well as within society. At all times they should be encouraged to appreciate and carry out their responsibilities and be given all the information, formation and freedom necessary for that task.

It is helpful, as I have already said, to regard the Extraordinary Synod and the Synod on the Laity as two parts of a single whole. Theologically they embrace the same ecclesiology and the same understanding of the Church as koinonia or communio. This approach has the advantage of rooting the life of the Church firmly in the mystery of God. The primary koinonia, from which the Church draws its life, is the Trinity itself. Each of the baptised is signed with the Trinity, not only to be incorporated individually into Christ, but also to be identified with the whole community of the redeemed who, being made one in Christ, are loved by the Father in the Spirit as the one body of Christ. This has social or communal consequences as profound as those which are personal and individual.

Father Walter Kaspar, in a lecture given before the Extraordinary Synod, pointed out that communio or koinonia:

> does not refer to the Church's structure, but to her essence, or, as the Council says, to her 'mysterium'. The aggiornamento of the Council consisted precisely in this: in contrast to the one-sided concentration on the visible and hierarchical form of the Church, it placed her mystery into the foreground again, her mystery which can only be grasped in faith.

Now the Church as koinonia is called into being by the word of God received and acted upon in faith.

The primary identity of lay people comes from their baptismal calling into the community of faith:

> From the fact of their union with Christ, the head, flows the lay person's right and duty to be apostles. Inserted as they are into the Mystical Body of Christ by baptism and strengthened by the power of the Holy Spirit in confirmation, it is by the Lord himself that they are assigned to the apostolate. (AA. N.2)

The baptismal character of the Christian life and mission, as already noted, is described as a sharing in the mission of Christ as prophet, priest and king. Perhaps surprisingly we have tended in the past when reflecting on the vocation and role of every Christian to concentrate almost exclusively on its priestly aspect – prayer, worship, offering of the Eucharist. The prophetic and kingly role of the whole people of God needs more careful attention and development. How do all the baptised, for instance, share in the prophetic and teaching mission of Christ, both within the community of faith and in the task of evangelisation? Is it exercised simply in the home or in the classroom of our Catholic schools? How should individuals witness to the faith and help spread it at local and national level and overseas? Are they to act individually or is there scope for organised action? In a similar way we need to ask how all the baptised are to be enabled to share in the kingly, governing or ordering mission of Christ (especially within the Church). Are they to be asked to undertake on their own initiative the task of sanctifying secular reality while being denied a responsible role in the life of their parish, deanery and diocese? These are difficult but important questions which require us to look closely at the structures and present practice of co-responsibility in the Church.

The consultation we made in England and Wales to prepare for the 1987 Synod confirmed what had already emerged clearly from our National Pastoral Congress in 1980, namely that Catholics in our two countries have a growing awareness of the fundamental importance of baptism. This has resulted partly from the experience of ecumenical dialogue and shared witness in Britain. The recognition of baptism administered in other churches is widely accepted as the foundation of the real but incomplete 'communion' which exists between the Christian churches. There undoubtedly exists a dynamic towards complete unity which arises out of baptism. It is this which gives hope and reassurance whenever setbacks are encountered along the road to unity. When Catholics grasp better the significance of baptism, their understanding and support for ecumenism grows rapidly.

Yet at the same time would I not be right in saying that the laity in general have not yet adequately grasped the implications of baptism as it applies to their life and activity *within* the Church? As already noted, many Catholics regard participation in the life of the Church as being a responsibility 'to help the priest': 'Just tell us what to do, Father, and we'll be there.' There is still much to be done to enable people to understand how their incorporation into the life of Christ gives them a direct share in his mission.

Father Walter Kaspar has this to say about the proper understanding of the Church:

> It has often been said that Vatican II itself is only a beginning. Karl Rahner even speaks of the beginning of a beginning. This becomes clear when we turn to a fourth dimension of communio, to the communio fidelium . . . The communio of the Churches and the collegiality of the bishops is rooted in a more fundamental communio, namely, the Church herself, the people of God. The Council texts speak expressly of this only in a few places. However, this meaning of communio is, in principle, theologically prepared through the doctrine of the common priesthood of all the baptised and of the active participation, the 'actuosa participatio' of the whole people of God which refers not only to the liturgy but to the whole life of the Church . . . This overcomes the idea of the Church as a 'societas inaequalis' [an unequal society]. The common identity of the people of God precedes all distinctions of offices, charisms and services . . . the interest of the laity and their readiness to share in responsibility is perhaps the most valuable and important contribution of the post-conciliar epoch . . . The ecclesiology of communio implies, after all, that there cannot co-exist in the Church active and passive members.

This is supremely important. It is crucial to understand that membership of the body of Christ involves every one of us personally and intensely in its life and activity. The expression 'active participation' was first used by Pope Pius XII to explain that the laity were not to be passive spectators of the Church's liturgy. Now we have begun to see that an active sharing in the liturgy necessarily involves an active sharing in the Church's mission. It is not simply a matter of borrowing a phrase from one aspect of the Church's life and applying it to another. Instead the words point to an essential link between the prayer life of the Church, the liturgy, and mission. Through the Church's liturgy the laity receive inspiration and guidance for their life and work. Word and sacrament are the indispensable foundation for apostolic action.

As the Decree on the Laity says:

> Only the light of faith and meditation on the Word of God can enable us to find everywhere and always the God 'in whom we live and exist' (Acts 17:28); only thus can we seek his will in everything, see Christ in all men, acquaintance or stranger, make sound judgements on the true meaning and value of temporal realities both in themselves and in relation to man's end. (Decree on the Laity, N.4).

In the past, ecumenical councils were often followed by the birth of new forms of religious life. The Second Vatican Council has given rise instead to a growing awareness of the role of the laity and to the development of new forms of active participation in the life of the Church. It is important to recognise that the power and creative energy of the Holy Spirit is still at work. In response to a rapidly changing world new forms of mission and ministry are taking shape. They need to be recognised and affirmed.

The Decree on the Apostolate of the Laity was uncompromising in the breadth of its vision and in the demands it made on lay people. It said this:

> Christ's redemptive work has as its main objective the salvation of men, but it involves as well a reconstruction of the whole temporal order. Therefore the Church has been sent not only to tell men about Christ and bring them his grace, but also to fill every corner of our world with the spirit of the Gospel and so bring it to its full perfection. The lay people, as they set about accomplishing this mission of the Church, work as apostles both in the Church and out in the world, among spiritual realities and among the things of the world. For even if there is a difference between these

two, the spiritual and the transient, in the one and only plan
of God they are so bound together that it is the whole
universe he intends to bring back to himself creating it
afresh in Christ. (Decree on the Laity, N.5)

It is hardly surprising that a mere twenty years has not sufficed
for the grandeur of this concept to be widely grasped and
translated into movements, organisations, structures. Yet it
has had its effect and we must be sensitive to what is already
being achieved throughout the world and, of course, in our
continent of Europe. It is a striking manifestation in practice
of koinonia, communio; there is a rich diversity of gifts within
the unity of Christ's body.

There has been, for example, an entirely new emphasis on
the creation of community in the post-conciliar Church. Mass
movements and vast impersonal parishes are giving way to
basic communities and small groups. Personal involvement
and the opportunity for response is welcomed. This tendency
can be seen in many places and reflects the new awareness of
the mystery which is Church.

There can be found, for example, in many parts of the
Church a much greater emphasis on developing the most
basic of all communities, the family. Increasingly we are
coming to realise the crucial role in human development and
happiness and its importance for the well-being of society.
Yet in many countries there is a major social crisis and new
destructive pressures on the family. In response there is in
many places a new apostolate of the family and an attempt to
bring out all the implications of what is meant by the domestic
church. The bishops of England and Wales have initiated a
three-year programme of pastoral renewal of family life. We
are at present in its early stages but the need is urgent.

Largely, of course, in the developing world, and particularly in Latin America and Africa, the post-conciliar Church
has witnessed the development of basic communities, a significant if sometimes controversial expression of the Council's
ecclesiology. In Europe there is nothing comparable to these
communities. It would seem that for us the development of
small groups and of the parish as a community of communities
offers the best hope of growth.

Undoubtedly among the signs of hope in the Church is the interest and pursuit of prayer and the things of the Spirit. The retreat movement, prayer-groups, the charismatic renewal, are very significant. The spread of the neo-catechumenate and the secular institutes, especially those with wider lay groups like the Focolare and the Grail, fill an obvious need in people for greater involvement in the life and mission of the Church, inspired by a deeper spiritual life. Some of these new movements have features which cause some concern; a careful pastoral discernment and oversight by the local bishop are needed.

The active apostolic movements with their long experience and specific areas of concern have a continuing role to fulfil. They have in the past been responsible for providing lay leaders whose influence was felt far outside their own organisations. Some of them have lost momentum and membership in recent years, but there is an urgent need to match the needs of the contemporary world with organised and specialised action. Catholic involvement in action and concern for others takes new forms today. In modern society there have sprung up professional groups to formulate and carry out a Christian response to pressing problems. Centres for medical ethics, groups formed to respond to the opportunities and challenge of modern means of communication, the Catholic associations of doctors, nurses, health workers, prison visitors and the like, are in their own way evidence of the creativity of the Spirit among the laity.

At the same time it has to be emphasised that membership of groups and movements is not essential for individual Catholics. Catholics have at all times and in every situation to witness to Christ and to fulfil their vocation in their daily lives. The vast majority of laity are not members of any organisations and play little or no part in the voluntary activity of their parishes. It is very important to make clear to people that the vocation and role of the laity is to be found principally in the conscientious discharge of family responsibilities, in the conduct of their daily lives at work and in society. It is here through their integrity, their sense of justice and fairness, their kindliness and concern, that they will make their surroundings a little more human, decent and welcoming.

Society may not seem to be sanctified or transformed to any remarkable degree by lives like these, but then we recall Christ's own description of the kingdom as mustard seed and leaven. We have not yet succeeded in persuading the laity about the reality of their role, of its necessity and of the spirituality from which it must spring.

This task is so demanding and daunting that it cannot be contemplated without radical renewal within the Church. This in turn, as noted elsewhere, depends upon a development of the spiritual life of the whole people of God. The reform of the liturgy by no means ensures its renewal nor that of the Church. There must be a constant effort to encourage prayer life and a deeper understanding and appreciation of the sacraments. This provides the inspiration and pattern for all apostolic activity. We have in so many ways neglected the roots of spirituality; we have not paid enough attention to the fostering of a spirituality for the laity that meets their hunger – often unacknowledged – for the things of God. We have not spelt out sufficiently how laity are to be equipped to fulfil their role in society and in the Church. How are we to make real in the lives of the whole people of God the inner mystery of Church which is communio?

That brings me to a final reflection. It has significance for renewal within the Church and for mission. Mission today must always, and because of the nature of the Church, necessarily involve dialogue. Pope Paul VI in his first encyclical 'Ecclesiam Suam' outlined a fourfold dialogue of the Church – with the world, with other faiths, with other Christians and internally, as he put it 'between members of a community founded upon love' (114). His insights were taken up and developed by the Second Vatican Council in such documents as: The Church in the Modern World; Missionary Activity and Non-Christian Religions; Ecumenism, the Church and Eastern Catholic Churches. In all these seminal documents dialogue is either explicitly referred to or is the presupposition implicit in them.

In theory at least dialogue could be one of many ways in which the Church relates to society and to others and conducts its own internal relationships. Pope Paul implicitly rejected two theoretical alternatives with regard to the world:

the Church might, in his words, 'content itself with conducting an enquiry into the evils current in secular society, condemning them publicly and fighting a crusade against them. On the other hand, it might approach secular society with a view to exercising a preponderant influence over it and subjecting it to a theocratic power' (78). Obviously there is little point to the first and little practical possibility of the second. However, we who have inherited the traditions of a Christian Europe must beware the temptation to long nostalgically for the restoration of Christendom, even locally, or to harbour the delusion that anything else is an evil to be combated.

On the contrary – and this is of immense importance – Pope Paul asserts that dialogue is necessitated:

> by the prevalent understanding of the relationship between the sacred and the profane. It is demanded by the pluralism of society and by the maturity man has reached in this day and age. Be he religious or not, his secular education has enabled him to think and speak and conduct a dialogue with dignity. (78)

There is no reason to believe that over the last twenty-five years the human race has significantly regressed. The pluralism of society is now even more pronounced and demands the dialogue suggested by Gaudium et Spes in which the Church is urged to listen and receive as much as it offers and speaks. Dialogue should not be mistaken for monologue. So whatever may have been true in the past, dialogue is today pre-eminently the style best suited to modern times.

Yet far from being merely a convenient tactic, dialogue for the Church has to be seen as 'modelled on the dialogue of salvation'. In that dialogue there is revelation and the individual's free response in the presence of which 'we dare not entertain any thoughts of external coercion' (75). The Council's affirmation of this understanding of divine revelation and religious freedom emphasises the Trinitarian dialogue by which God unfolds himself to man and also the free response of man, whose enquiry into truth demands 'the aid of teaching . . . communication and dialogue' (3). So dialogue corresponds to the pattern of the divine economy, and it respects both God's revelation and the dignity and freedom of the human person.

To lay such stress on dialogue might seem to undermine the understanding we used to have of mission, which was seen largely as a matter of proclamation and witness. It is clear that dialogue in itself is not directly aimed at 'conversion to the true faith' – at least not as its first objective. Dialogue is none the less a way of evangelising, a first step, to show the richness of God's revelation. It is possible to resolve the apparent tension at a deeper level.

The mission of the Church and of all the Church's members is not, in a sense, their own mission at all; it is Christ's mission and is, therefore, God's mission. At a particular moment Christ appointed the apostles and their successors to carry on his mission on earth, but he did not then simply depart and leave the rest to them. He still conducts his mission now and his headship of the Church is effectively exercised through the outpouring on us of the Holy Spirit. Without that outpouring we would not be his body and he could not carry out his mission. So it was not a once-for-all act of the past; it is an ongoing Pentecost.

But dialogue is our human mode in particular, by which we enable Christ to carry out his mission. We do not as yet possess the whole truth – all Christian history is a gradual exploration of it under the inspiration of the Spirit. The Church is constantly developing in its understanding of revelation (Dei Verbum, 5). And so dialogue is our proper mode of operation in order to enlarge our understanding and deepen our awareness as conscious instruments of Christ's mission.

The presence of the kingdom and of uncovenanted – and sometimes surprising – grace in the world, means that we have to learn as well as teach, listen as well as speak. Respect for others, recognition of the 'seeds of the Gospel' planted throughout human society, consciousness that the whole of creation is made from the beginning in the Word, all lead us to a deeper and truer understanding of the world and the Church, of its mission and the role of the laity in it. Gaudium et Spes provided us with all the elements for present reflection and future action. The world to which we are sent in God's name is already God's and fitfully reflects his truth, goodness and beauty. It is for those consciously committed to union with Christ to be at the world's service and in dialogue with it so that the fullness of truth may be gradually revealed and the world renewed in love.

10

The Experience of Ecumenism

The movement for Christian unity engages the attention and support of the Catholic Church at this time. Pope John Paul II addressing the Roman Curia on June 28th, 1985 said:

> Every particular Church, every bishop ought to have solicitude for unity and ought to promote the ecumenical movement . . . The search for unity and ecumenical concern are a necessary dimension of the whole of the Church's life. Everything can and must contribute to it. I have already asked on more than one occasion that the re-establishment of unity among all Christians really be considered one of the pastoral priorities. We are *committed* together with our brothers of the other churches and ecclesial communities in the ecumenical movement . . . This movement is stirred by the Holy Spirit and I consider myself to be profoundly responsible in its regard.

The work for Christian unity, so emphatically endorsed by the present Pope, is of course rooted in scripture. Our Lord said at the Last Supper:

> I do not pray for these only, but also for those who believe in me through their word, that they may all be one; even as thou, Father, art in me, and I in thee, that they also may be in us, so that the world may believe that thou hast sent me. (John 17:20–21)

Confronted by almost immediate conflict within the early Christian community in Corinth, St Paul wrote:

> I appeal to you . . . that there be no dissensions among you, but that you be united in the same mind and the same judgment. For it has been reported to me by Chloe's people that there is quarrelling among you, my brethren. What I mean is that each one of you says, 'I belong to Paul,' or 'I belong to Apollos,' or 'I belong to Cephas,' or 'I belong to Christ.' Is Christ divided? (1 Cor. 1:10–13)

The present situation was described by the Second Vatican Council in its Decree on Ecumenism:

> One cannot charge with the sin of separation those who at present are born into those communities and in them are brought up in the faith of Christ and the Catholic Church accepts them with respect and affection as brothers. For men who believe in Christ and have been properly baptised share some communion, though imperfect, with the Catholic Church. Without doubt, the differences that exist in varying degrees between them and the Catholic Church – whether in doctrine and sometimes in discipline, or concerning the structure of the Church – do indeed create many obstacles, sometimes serious ones, to full ecclesiastical communion. The ecumenical movement is striving to overcome those obstacles. (Unitatis Redintegratio, N.3)

The Council rejoiced in the close relationship and remarkable unity between all the baptised. We can thank God and celebrate that unity which is created by our baptism in Christ. For the Catholic Church it was a Copernican revolution when the decision was taken not to baptise conditionally those Christians seeking full communion. Recognition of a common baptism marked a decisive stage on the journey together towards unity.

It has to be said immediately, of course, that this communion and unity is as yet incomplete as the Council recognised. There is but one baptism but there is not as yet one faith. Christians still disagree over what they believe and do not accept the same Church order, and especially so in matters concerned with ministry and the exercise of authority. They do not constitute one Church. The continuing structural diversity is clearly indicative of the present lack of unity. But the Holy Spirit is at work.

To make progress in unity we must approach each other in openness and with total honesty. We must declare the positions we hold and hold fast to what is essential. Whatever difficulties the future may hold, and however slow the pace, we should rejoice in our real but imperfect communion. Unity is gift and is being offered to us at this present time; it is also growth and that too is happening. Growing pains are inevitable but are a sign of change. To the doubters and the discouraged I offer a story of real hope.

I want now to describe a journey. It is a pilgrimage presently being undertaken by more than thirty churches. It has some features of more than passing interest to all who seek a way forward towards the goal of full organic Christian unity. It is a journey still in progress; the route has now been chosen; there will certainly be difficult terrain ahead but we have committed ourselves and are hopeful of the outcome. It is important to describe the process in some detail because the means chosen are themselves significant for the ecumenical movement. Here I have with permission made use of accounts of the Inter-Church Process written by the Secretary of the bishops' conference of England and Wales and already published in *Briefing*, the Conference's official documentation service.

For many years progress towards Christian unity in Britain was measured by success in removing prejudice and creating means of cooperation. Great emphasis was placed on what might be called organisational ecumenism. The question, for example, most frequently posed to the Bishops' Conference of England and Wales in the past decade has been: 'When is the Catholic Church going to join the British Council of Churches?' For some this had become almost an end in itself. The National Pastoral Congress in 1980 revealed among many Catholics considerable enthusiasm for full membership of the Council of Churches as proof of ecumenical sincerity. There remained hesitation in the bishops' conference, not about ecumenical concern but about how best to express it and make it effective. Was Council membership the best way ahead in the years after the Second Vatican Council?

The papal visit of 1982 was rich in symbolic gestures of Christian friendship, respect and reconciliation. The world still remembers the historic encounter between the Archbishop of Canterbury and the Pope, followed by a meeting with all Church leaders. There was an atmosphere of euphoria which was almost immediately dissipated when the Covenant proposals broke down. The Catholic Church played no part in the final stages of that initiative. It had involved the Anglican and Protestant churches of Britain and its failure was keenly felt. It was clear that a radically different approach was called for; one which would involve all the churches in a return to basic considerations.

In 1983 the Easter Conference of the Roman Catholic bishops of England and Wales came to the conclusion that what lay at the heart of ecumenism was the question of ecclesiology, the understanding of the nature of the Church. It had become very obvious that the word 'Church' was being made to carry many meanings and mask many differences. Our 1984 January study week concentrated on those questions and, significantly, leaders of other Christian churches were invited to participate in part of that meeting. A long weekend of recollection and prayer together at Canterbury in the spring of 1984 paved the way for two important decisions. One was taken at the British Council of Churches Spring Assembly which resolved 'to consult the member Churches and other Christian bodies on their readiness to share in a process of prayer, reflection and debate together, centred on the nature and purpose of the Church in the light of its calling in and for the world'. The second was taken when our Catholic bishops' conference that Easter resolved 'to collaborate with the British Council of Churches in the preparation of a major conference in 1987 to consider the nature of the Church in the light of the Lima document, ARCIC and relevant documents of Vatican II'.

Out of this arose an Inter-Church Process entitled 'Not Strangers but Pilgrims', which is probably unique in its scope and its involvement of a wide popular constituency. This has been planned in three stages, two of which have already been completed. The outcome of this three-year process should be the working out of new proposals for 'ecumenical instruments' to help serve the churches in the search for that unity for which Christ prayed.

From our deliberations has emerged a twin principle to which I shall return. It is that any ecumenical instruments we devise for future ecumenical progress must help the churches to act together and not be an extrinsic agency set up to act on behalf of the churches and that these instruments must be firmly rooted in the authority structure of each participating Church. We did not set out with such clear-cut concepts; they are the fruit of our pilgrimage. They will provide the orientation for the next stage of our journey. It is interesting to recall in a little more detail how we progressed from the formal resolutions of the BCC and the Bishops' Conference to where we are today.

The first phase of 'Not Strangers but Pilgrims' embraced three levels. There was, at popular level, an attempt to involve 'people in the pews' who belonged to the participating churches. It took the form of a Lent 1986 course devoted to the theme: 'What on earth is the Church for?' It was, astonishingly, accepted by more than fifty local radio stations and it is estimated that more than a million people took part. The findings of those discussion groups are now published in a book, *Views from the Pews*. They reveal that people believe that the purpose of the Church is 'to worship God' and 'to give a Gospel witness in our society'. But the questions also reached into people's hopes for unity between the churches, which were remarkably high. This 'popular level' of the first phase was also addressed to all local councils of churches and local ecumenical projects in England and Wales. Their responses too are included in *Views from the Pews*. They put forward their own experience as a rich source of achievement and reflection not perhaps being fully appreciated or utilised by the wider Church communities.

Phase One of 'Not Strangers but Pilgrims' also addressed a more formal question to the leaders – or in some cases the headquarters – of all the participating churches: 'In your tradition and experience, how do you understand the nature and purpose of your Church [or Churches when the national body is a federation of local congregations]: (a) in relation to other Christian denominations and (b) as together we share in God's mission to the world?' The responses to this question received from the participating churches have also been published in a book: *Reflections: how churches view their life and mission.*

Finally, Phase One has also gathered the views of many other groups and bodies not formally part of the Inter-Church Process. The views of young people, the house church movement, women's groups, the National Association of Christian Centres and Networks, some Third World agencies, views from Christian churches in other parts of the world and some of the findings of international dialogues like ARCIC, all these are given expression in a third book called *Observations.*

All three books were published jointly by the British Council of Churches and the Catholic Truth Society. They bring together three voices: the so-called 'grass-roots', those with particular responsibility for leadership and unity in the churches and those who take 'alternative viewpoints' through conviction or experience. These three voices need each other; they should be heard and heeded by each other. They have rarely been given the opportunity to do so.

The next phase of the Process involved a series of major conferences, three at national level in England, Scotland and Wales, culminating in a meeting of all three nations at Swanwick. An Inter-Church Group laid the foundations for these conferences by reflecting on the findings of the original enquiry and producing a series of questions under three headings, on the nature, the purpose and the unity of the Church. A selection of these questions will serve as an indication of how the conferences were to tackle the ecumenical agenda.

On the nature of the Church, for example: 'In our traditions and ecumenical experience how do we understand the universality of the Church? Does the phrase, "the body of Christ", indicate a spiritual reality only, or does it have visible characteristics by which it can be recognised?' And inevitably the question is faced about the nature and exercise of authority: 'In our traditions and ecumenical experience, how is the truth God communicates to his people discerned and expressed in the community of faith? How do the forms and structures of Church life enable us to be aware of new light from God and to be faithful to the Gospel?' On the purpose of the Church, one question asked how greater cooperation between the churches could be brought about in worship and prayer, evangelisation, serving human need and shaping culture and society. Discussion on the unity of the Church was divided into two sections: the first to do with our vision of unity (for example, 'How do our different understandings of the nature and purpose of the Church shape our different visions of unity?') and the second concerned with means towards unity (for example, 'What are the chief lessons to be learned from local ecumenical projects and sponsoring bodies about the possible means for closer cooperation between the Churches at regional and national levels?').

The three spring conferences each furthered the process. The English gathering at Nottingham reviewed the whole of the agenda. Discussions brought to the surface some of the substantial differences of opinion that exist on matters such as the rite of sacraments in the Christian life, the shape and exercise of authority in a Christian community, the priorities of mission and purpose in today's society and so on. Yet the conference was able to give a resounding 'yes' to the fundamental question: 'Do we have sufficient unity between us to enable us to continue this process despite the differences and diversity which also exist?'

The Welsh conference at Bangor was described as an example of 'spiritual ecumenism'. At its conclusion delegates were saying that the Inter-Church Process itself was an 'ecumenical instrument', a way by which the churches could successfully come together to grow in understanding, cooperation and commitment.

In Scotland, at St Andrews, ecumenical confrontation was the keynote. Set positions were clearly stated. Representatives explained with considerable theological precision and force the beliefs and reservations they held. Issues of authority were once again near the top of the agenda, as was an insistence to look for far more details in any initial proposals about how the churches might organise their relationships, about what sort of ecumenical instruments are needed. Here, as elsewhere, the different patterns of authority were noted: the authority of the individual, the authority of the congregation or whole community, the authority of the designated leadership or college.

The themes which emerged from the final reports of these national conferences were central to the Inter-Church Process. How do the various participants understand the Church, especially in relationship to the kingdom of God and to the world? Can the term 'koinonia' help us to grow together in our understanding of ecumenism since it gives priority to God and to the way in which each Christian is drawn into participation or communion in his life? Out of this communio arises our mission, for we are sent to cooperate in the creative work of the Father, the redemptive work of the Son and the sanctifying work of the Holy Spirit. Does this perspective help the Christian churches in Britain to see how they can work together more closely? Can we find a solid basis on which to move towards more practical cooperation directly between the churches, at every level? And can we move from there towards deeper commitment, one to another?

Thus the scene was set for the Swanwick conference at the end of August 1987. In the event that conference came to be described by Archbishop Runcie of Canterbury as 'historic', and by Archbishop Worlock of Liverpool as 'momentous'. The BBC Religious Correspondent described the atmosphere as 'electric'. Yet it was a meeting of some 330 experienced conference-goers and Church leaders, people not given to passing enthusiasms, more accustomed to assessing consequences and reacting with considerable caution. So plainly something special took place. I believe myself it was one of those rare occasions when the Council Decree on Ecumenism took flesh and was seen to be alive and full of hope and promise. It was an experience of real but incomplete communion or koinonia. The meeting began on quite a pedestrian note. There were two days devoted to theological and doctrinal debate on the nature of the Church and its mission.

The second part of the conference considered, on the basis

of these theological discussions, how the churches might best work and grow together. The conference discussed structures, organisations or practical arrangements to serve and develop relationships between the churches. These are the so-called 'ecumenical instruments'. But the conference was also an experience of prayer and silence. Each day we prayed together, the Eucharist was celebrated according to the rites and disciplines of the participating churches. This experience of shared worship had a major influence on the work of the conference. The Catholic discipline on inter-communion, when explained, also played its own part in demonstrating our baptismal unity, our partial communion and our longing for full organic union.

The issues throughout were confronted with determination and a good deal of straight talking. Some delegates initially were worried about how Roman Catholics might react but nothing is more satisfying than to see genuine theological dialogue at the heart of the ecumenical process. There can be no way forward in doctrinal fudge and compromise. We bring to the dialogue and the work for unity all that we are and all the richness of our inheritance. The truth, and only the truth, will set us free. Insistence on theological discussion is the major contribution Catholics can make to the Inter-Church Process. Those considerations were to shape our response.

As the Swanwick meeting proceeded it became quite clear that the others were looking to us, the Roman Catholic representatives, to declare ourselves. If the process was to have a future it needed a clear sign from us of our intentions. The English group met and agreed that I should express to the conference our approval of the process. It was extraordinary to witness the effect on others and to see a routine meeting, as it were, catch fire. I have subsequently described myself as being 'Balaam's ass' because what I said was nothing new. I believed myself to be expressing the mind of the Council in its Decree on Ecumenism. I did not say anything that has not been put in general terms a hundred and one times before. But there is always the right time, the right audience, the 'kairos'.

What apparently caught the imagination of the conference was the use of the word 'commitment'. I said:

First I hope that our Roman Catholic delegates at this Conference will recommend to members of our Church that we move now quite deliberately from a situation of cooperation to one of commitment to each other. By 'commitment to each other' I mean that we commit ourselves to praying and working together for Church unity and to acting together, both nationally and locally, for evangelisation and mission.

I was concerned to express the truth that the Catholic Church is committed to the process of achieving Christian unity. Commitment is a word used in a technical sense in ecumenical matters.

Professional ecumenists speak of five stages in ecumenical relationships. This is to omit an important reality which is that of partial communion which perhaps is best understood as underlying all that we are and do as Christians. The five stages however are a useful aid to understanding how unity develops:

1. we are in competition
2. we co-exist
3. we cooperate
4. we commit ourselves
5. we are in communion.

The significance of a deliberate move from cooperation to commitment can never be underestimated. The Pope has made it clear that the Church has now made that deliberate move which I expressed at Swanwick. It is, however, something which makes considerable demands upon us. Father Michael Jackson, who is secretary of the Bishops' Committee for Christian Unity of our Conference, has recently described those demands which he believes amount to a real conversion. He writes in *Priests and People* on 'What happened at Swanwick?':

Conversion is a process of change at three levels: a change of perception, a reassessment of the value of what we do and a new pattern of behaviour. Roman Catholics in this country are well aware of what happens when a change of behaviour is made without a new perception and a new evaluation of our needs: the problems we have with the Sacrament of Penance bear ample witness to this folly.

Growth into unity involves a renewal of our perceptions and a new evaluation of where we have arrived on the ecumenical pilgrimage. Without this conversion the challenge to move further on the road to unity with whole hearts and clear minds cannot be met.

The primary motive and aim is the proclamation of the kingdom. But the growth in truth that such a proclamation announces must be reflected in the lives of those who bring the Good News. In other words, the truth that we proclaim should be seen in our own relations with our Christian brothers and sisters. In the Cardinal's words we have a signal that the Roman Catholic Church is resolved not to remain in the realm of merely cooperative ecumenical efforts that perpetuate ecclesial parallelism; he is declaring a commitment to grow together through evangelisation and mission, into a fuller experience of unity and truth.

Commitment, I need hardly add, is a penultimate stage. The goal is communion. Whatever ecumenical instrument we eventually fashion in Britain must help us grow towards full organic unity. At Swanwick I said:

By full communion I mean that 'koinonia', that fellowship, that one-ness in the body of Christ, of which the essential elements were already outlined in the Acts of the Apostles . . . 'be true to the teaching of the apostles, the breaking of bread, to fellowship and prayer'. That followed the passage describing the descent of the Holy Ghost on the apostles. From this followed the task of evangelisation and action resulting from concern for those in need. In a full 'communion' we recognise, of course, that there will not be uniformity but legitimate diversity. It is often not stressed sufficiently that even within the Roman Catholic Church there is considerable diversity.

I realise that not all members of the Roman Catholic Church have yet grasped and interiorised this vision of the Church. The major theological advance since the Council in our understanding of the Church has been the growing awareness that the Church is best described in terms of koinonia or communion. It is the key to ecumenical advance. It helps restore baptism to its rightful place in our understanding of the Christian life; it adds an irresistible dynamism to the search for Christian unity; it explains how separated Christians are in real but partial communion and how that partial separation has to be overcome in patient and untiring dialogue; it is an essential concept if we are to avoid what Michael Jackson calls 'the all-or-nothing approach to ecumenism which does not allow for growth'. I am personally convinced that while mission is of the essence of the Church and so rightly formed a large part of the concern of the churches at Swanwick, equally important for the Church is the exploration of the mystery of God, a deeper, shared quest for the truth that we all directly experience in koinonia. It is an exploration to be advanced in common reflection and prayer. Furthermore the Catholic Church will contribute to the ecumenical dialogue its official teaching on matters of faith and morals. We would not be true to ourselves if we failed to do this. Thus the words of the Anglican Roman Catholic International Commission at the end of its introduction to the Final Report were, from a Catholic point of view, very encouraging: 'Full visible communion between our two Churches cannot be achieved without mutual recognition of sacraments and ministry, together with the common acceptance of a universal primacy, at one with the episcopal college in the service of koinonia' (ARCIC, Introduction, N.9).

Mention of direct experience brings out a further aspect of our mutual concerns throughout the Inter-Church Process. From start to finish we were conscious that Christian unity as a gift from God must be rooted in the experience of koinonia or fellowship at local and personal level. It is never an administrative arrangement, a mere mechanism for conducting joint business. That is why we tried to involve people in the pew from the outset, why we were careful to move from local to national and from national to international discussion and why we at all stages gave ourselves to prayer as well as to discussion. There will never be authentic evolution of Church unity which does not arise from a kind of multi-faceted unity at local level. Whatever else our future ecumenical instruments might do, they must not only foster ecumenical relationships locally but also action in the locality and a shared spiritual experience between local congregations.

Some of the ideas were expressed in a Final Declaration read from pulpits in all the participating churches. Drawn up overnight, as is the custom in such conferences, the declaration is admittedly imperfect but it manages to seize the essential spirit of the whole process. It states that 'this, the broadest assembly of British and Irish Churches ever to meet in these islands has reached a common mind'. It goes on:

> we met, we listened, we talked, we worshipped, we prayed, we sat in silence, deeper than words. Against the background of so much suffering and sinfulness in our society we were reminded of our call to witness that God was in Christ reconciling the world to himself . . . We now declare together our readiness to commit ourselves to each other under God. Our earnest desire is to become more fully, in his own time, the one Church of Christ, united in faith, communion, pastoral care and mission. Such unity is the gift of God. With gratitude we have truly experienced this gift, growing amongst us in these days. We affirm our openness to this growing unity in obedience to the Word of God, so that we may fully share, hold in common, and offer to the world those gifts which we have received and still hold in separation.

Who can say what the end of this process will be? One step at a time and Swanwick has been a very decisive one, but the pilgrimage continues. Churches will make their final decisions about the new ecumenical instruments in the spring of 1989. The pathway for these new instruments has been cleared also by the fact that all present British Council of Churches contracts of employment with executive staff will end in the summer of 1990. The new arrangements should come into operation at that time. New horizons are opening up.

A final word on possible new models. The Swanwick Conference did not envisage one ecumenical instrument but an instrument for each nation, England, Scotland and Wales and an international one for Britain and Ireland. These future structures would in no sense assume an identity independent of the participating churches. They would enable the churches to take action together and would not have authority to speak on their behalf. All authority would remain within the churches. That is an essential principle to which I have already referred.

All of this will constitute the agenda for the next stage of our Inter-Church Process. We are open to the movement of the Spirit while remaining entirely faithful to our inheritance. As Roman Catholics we cannot undertake initiatives or take decisions except in complete harmony with Peter and the universal Church. Yet we are also conscious that we are privileged to participate in an ecumenical venture of considerable significance for the future of Christian unity. Many features of our shared pilgrimage in Great Britain and Ireland are unique but they have, I believe, a value for Christian ecumenism in general.

I have elsewhere expressed my conviction that this shared pilgrimage though blessed by God and guided by his Holy Spirit will have to tread the way of the cross. We need the Church to be visibly one so that the body of Christ may be appropriately incarnate and the Church might fulfil without ambiguity its mission to be universal sacrament of salvation, effecting what it signifies. The world needs the guarantee that the word of God is being authentically interpreted and the sacraments of Christ validly conferred. We need a united Church so that all the richness of Christ might be constantly available and shared by all and so that a united voice might bear witness to the message of Christ. It is singularly important that the world should know where to find the Church of Christ.

For Catholics, as we commit ourselves humbly but irrevocably to the work for unity, the theological position is clear and has to be maintained in all charity. As Cardinal Willebrands reiterated as recently as May 1987: 'the one and genuine Church of God is found in the Catholic Church'. At the same time we assert with him 'that the Church of God extends though lacking fullness, beyond the Catholic Church'.

What this means, how it is to be reconciled in the future remains to be further explored and resolved.

11

The Local Church of the Future

The pastoral reality of the Church today is very diverse and we know little of what is happening in each of the five continents. A starting point is the recognition that the parish and the diocese vary not only from continent to continent, country to country, but also within a nation and region. And parishes are different even within a city or town. An effective model in one situation cannot simply be transplanted into another environment.

In its necessary diversity, the local church must respect the unity of the whole Church and the tradition it has received. There are, and will continue to be, other ways of being Church in the world. Experience, especially from Latin America and Africa, will do much to enrich European thinking about the local church. It seems important to me that new developments should be sensitive to the theological tradition of the Church and especially in respect of its sacramental system. We now need to look afresh at the teaching of the Council in the light of subsequent experience and to see in what ways the new Code of Canon Law applies that teaching to concrete situations and provides opportunity for legitimate development.

We have no experience in Britain of basic Christian communities as they are found in Latin America and Africa. In our situation, however, and in much of Europe and North America, small groups are emerging and should be further encouraged as basic cells within the parish. These are not an alternative to the parish but help it to be more effective and creative.

In general then, without ruling out other developments, I am using here the term 'local church' to refer to the parish. The parish is defined in the new Code of Canon Law (Canon 515.s1) as 'a certain community of Christ's faithful stably established within a particular Church [that is, the diocese] whose pastoral care, under the authority of the diocesan bishop, is entrusted to a parish priest as its proper pastor'. There is no definition in Canon Law nor any treatment in the Council document of basic Christian communities. These are subsequent developments. But I think much of what I have to say is relevant to them.

It is not enough, however, to reflect on the parish in isolation from the world. The local church has to be seen in its setting within the secular community of which it is part, subject to the same social pressures and influences. A study of the parish has to take into account the world it has to evangelise. Its members are affected in so many ways by their neighbours. We cannot plan a pastoral strategy without consideration of the factors which are changing secular society today. Most of us will remember, for example, what the advent of television did to parish life. We know the effect on religious life of the movement for women's liberation. We experience the pastoral effects of that breakdown in marriage which has become an epidemic in western society.

New technology in communication, the coming of the Age of Information, the introduction of microchip technology, advances in transport systems, population trends, all these are not simply secular or irrelevant to the study of the parish. They are likely to revolutionise our society, its social patterns and the world of work and leisure and will affect the way we experience life in our local church.

Just as important as these tangible changes is the atmosphere in which we live, the attitudes held by people generally. From a European point of view, it would seem that there are grounds for hope as well as reasons for concern.

In a time of accelerating change and a good deal of moral confusion, there is evidence that many people are seeking new answers to the fundamental questions of life. Who am I? What is life for? Where am I going? There is in other words a search for the meaning and purpose of human life. In many cases the person and the words of Jesus Christ still speak to the people of our time; they still have the power to attract. There is also a desire to learn about prayer and the principles of the spiritual life. There is also, especially among the young, a thirst for justice and for peace, a new and growing sense of solidarity with the oppressed, the poor and the deprived. This is linked with a recognition of human dignity and rights.

There is, unhappily, evidence also of deep-rooted malaise in our society. It is an age of unbelief, or, rather, a turning from the true God to the worship of false gods. We make for ourselves idols of power, possessions and pleasure. We tolerate a world where peace is secured mainly by the threat of mutually-assured destruction by nuclear weapons; we are still tempted to settle conflicts by force of arms; militants assert their claims or promote their causes by urban terrorism or guerrilla war; we can even turn sporting rivalry into a hideous carnage. We tolerate a society where the rich nations get richer and the poor poorer; we are loath to reform our international trading patterns; we prefer occasional emergency aid to long-term development; we favour the strong and take advantage of the weak. We tolerate a society which has put the pursuit of pleasure and self-fulfilment above the demands of duty and responsibility; we have turned our backs on the disciplines of love; we have devalued fidelity and commitment; we experience the decay of family life. The process is sadly all too familiar in human history. We turn from the living God; we begin to worship false gods; we end by being destroyed by them.

It comes as no surprise, surely, that the Church which lives at the heart of the human community should experience difficulties and tensions at this time. There are some who talk of crisis and mean simply danger. When I use the word it is in the biblical sense of being faced with a choice, of making a judgement which will, in its turn, judge us. Is it not true that we can see in the Church today, both in its priests and its people, a crisis of the head and a crisis of the heart? The crisis of the head is to do with faith. Many experience uncertainty and confusion about the content of the faith and how to express it in terms intelligible to people today.

We also experience it in trying to understand the Church and its nature and function in our day. Many feel alienated from the Church as an institution, not seeing in it the body of Christ. Others experience the Church primarily as 'problem' since they cannot see in the Church the vision entrusted to us by Christ our Lord. The radical temptation is then to dismantle the Church as we have it and to seek to fashion a reformed Church responding to the felt needs of today's believers.

To do this, however, is to run the risk of setting up a man-made sect or a temple made by human hands. It would ignore the fact that today is only one stage of the pilgrimage of the Lord's people. It could well result in cutting ourselves off from the rest of the Church of the past and the future. We must be sensitive to the Spirit of God speaking to us in creation and in human history, but we have to accept that it is the same Spirit who presided at Pentecost at the birth of the Church and has guided it ever since. There is the dialectic of the Spirit in which the Church is caught up in every age and every continent. This is more than a matter for the mind. It calls for an opening of the heart to what the Spirit is saying not only to ourselves but to all the churches at this time.

The crisis of the heart is to do with our emotions and affections, with the relationships we create and with the attitudes we have to others, especially to those who claim authority over us. We are undoubtedly affected not only by the permissiveness of society and the breakdown of family life, but also by our heightened expectations. In our day there is increased emphasis on personal fulfilment, emotional development, effective formation. Many priests experience, certainly more so than in the past, a sense of dissatisfaction, a lack of fulfilment, human loneliness. This has led some to advocate the abandonment of celibacy, but the problem is more profound. Marriage is not itself the answer; indeed it is part of the contemporary problem. Although there are good arguments in favour of married clergy, none the less we should not too easily conclude that marriage will resolve the problems to which celibacy can give rise. The crisis of the heart extends to the whole Church. The people of God need a spirituality that is meaningful and satisfying. The crisis is manifest too in the negative reaction against authority in all its forms which is felt in the Church as well as in society. This has led to the creation of factions, sects and disruptive movements within the Church and to a disregard, in practice, for the role and responsibility of the pastor in the Church.

How are we to find and express the mind and the heart of Christ for his Church today? Since it is clearly not possible for us to re-invent the Church but necessary instead to ponder the mystery we already live, we can turn to the Dogmatic Constitution on the Church, Lumen Gentium, to discover how the pastors of the Church in council describe the inner dynamism and vital structure of the particular church, the diocese, and the local community of the parish. Paragraph 26 is the place where the Constitution speaks to us explicitly about the local church. There we read that the Church of Christ 'is truly present in all legitimate local congregations of the faithful which, united with their pastors, are themselves called churches in the New Testament'. The faithful are gathered together by the preaching of the Gospel and the mystery of the Lord's Supper. Here Christ is present and because of him 'the one, holy, catholic and apostolic Church gathers together'. The Eucharist is the Church at its most manifest; it is the worship of the whole Christ, head and members. We become members of that body through baptism. Without baptism and the Eucharist there can be no true Christian community; without the bishop, as 'vicar and ambassador of Christ' there can be no Eucharist and no community. Around his altar is gathered the particular church which is the diocese. The parish priests share the ministry of the bishop and 'make him present in a certain sense in the individual local congregations of the faithful . . . As they sanctify and govern under the bishop's authority that part of the Lord's flock entrusted to them, they make the universal Church visible in their own locality' (N.28).

Each manifestation of the universal Church in a local situation, each parish or community within the diocese, makes real that koinonia, that communion, to which the Holy Spirit calls us so insistently today. We should be able to find in each local church not only koinonia but all the qualities which are derived from it and which became part of the vocabulary of the Council: collegiality, diakonia, co-responsibility, subsidiarity, dialogue and others. The local parish should be a church of communion and community, a sharing church, a church which respects its members and consults them seriously, a missionary and evangelising church, a caring and serving church, a church which is in constant dialogue with neighbouring Christian churches and engaged with them in common Christian witness.

It is painfully obvious that there is a wide gap between the ideal and the real. How then is the local church, the parish, to be renewed? How can it best serve the deep spiritual needs of the local people of God? After all, if it is at local level that the universal Church is made visible, the faithful should be able to find there what they need for mind, heart and spirit. The parish community, somehow or another, has to give people experientially some awareness and understanding of the ultimate meaning and purpose of their lives. It has to help them to interpret their experience, to find God, to seek his kingdom here and hereafter.

To achieve this the parish community has to be able to allow people to relate to each other and to their pastor at a personal level and with freedom and trust. This is usually impossible within our contemporary parishes because of their size and the uneven social, intellectual and cultural mix to be found there. The first most obvious and necessary step is to develop within the parish a host of smaller natural groupings or associations. It is here that a deeper, more personal spiritual formation can be carried out, that worship and prayer can be given new life and that action can be more effectively planned and carried out.

This is hardly a revolutionary proposal. The need for some such strategy is everywhere acknowledged. It must be admitted however that while the principle might have universal importance, the realisation of it will be different in different cultures. It may be that in some situations territorial groupings of believers, the historic parish communities, are not the answer. We must not, however, do violence to our traditions. We cannot, and need not in many cases, free ourselves from the buildings, the organisations and the structures of the past. They need not weigh us down. They can be adapted and renewed. The creation of smaller, more human-size communities does not in fact necessarily imply the dismantling of the parish or its abandonment but its transformation.

I would argue strongly from within my own experience that the parish can be given new life if it is regarded and organised as a community of communities, as a resource centre and a focus for the coordination of pastoral and missionary activities. It is a mistake in my view to adopt arbitrary and simplistic solutions and strategies. From the basic cell up to the universal Church certain tasks and missions can be accomplished effectively only at certain levels. Not everything can be achieved by the parish, deanery or diocese. Some things are only possible at the level of bishops' conferences and yet others by the universal Church. We have to decide how best to achieve any pastoral goal and maintain in good order all the structures we need.

I would agree that small groups and basic communities are vital for personal and spiritual formation. In talking to such groups, whether they be family groups, prayer groups, associations of lay apostolic action, professional groups, neighbourhood or house mass groups, I usually lay stress on three words: prayer, faith, action. Small groups are an effective school for prayer. We have never devoted enough time and energy to the task of teaching people how to pray, creating the right environment for prayer and encouraging the constant practice of prayer. This would meet a great hunger in our people. The example and commitment of the pastor will be decisive. The small groups, the basic communities should be rooted in prayer and shaped by prayer. And the supreme prayer of any group, any community, must be the Mass.

At the same time the faith of the individual and any community must be nourished by an attentive reading of the scriptures and by shared study and the prayerful discernment of what the present situation demands of the Christian believer. I see immense value in that well-tested pastoral technique first formulated by Joseph Cardijn, the see-judge-act method. Seeing and judging is to lead to action. Pastoral apathy and inertia, which is content with maintenance, has to give way to an urgent sense of mission. I know of no continent where there is not need for well-thought-out, well-planned, ecumenically-based programmes of evangelisation involving the whole people of God and inspired and maintained by the local church. There is a danger instead of clericalising the laity, making them a volunteer force for the benefit of maintaining Church structures and initiatives.

I want to make three points. I shall first reflect on the mission and ministry of lay people; secondly I shall suggest ways in the future of exercising responsibility within the parish community; thirdly I shall consider the lay ministries and their relationship to the local church.

It is in my view a mistake to begin reflection on the role of laity in the Church by starting from the shortage of priests. This shortage is not as yet universally critical. Everyone knows the problems experienced in some countries not only about vocations to the priesthood but, even more dramatically, about the decline of vocations to religious life among women. We know also that there are real difficulties arising from the ageing of the existing clergy. Yet the response to the scarcity of priests should not be to ask what the laity can do without the ministry of an ordained priest. Since we affirm the centrality of the Eucharist, we must instead consider, and urgently, how best to call forth from the community sufficient candidates for the priesthood. We shall soon arrive at the situation (if we have not in many places already reached it) when bishops will have to select from within the local community persons of appropriate experience, age and integrity to be ordained to the priesthood. They may indeed be married men. Now I, for one, value very much the tradition of celibacy in the Latin Church and would very much wish to see it preserved. I do, however, foresee the ordaining to the priesthood of married men in certain parts of the world as the only way to bring the sacraments of the Eucharist and reconciliation to the people. The essential qualities required in such a person are already listed for us in St Paul's first letter to Timothy (3:1–7).

Instead, then, of beginning from the scarcity of priests, the right theological starting-point for any consideration of the role of the laity in the Church are the sacraments of baptism and confirmation. Through baptism we all share in the priestly, prophetic and kingly role of Christ. Through confirmation we are equipped to be witnesses in the world to the Gospel. Reflecting on these two sacraments we are led to certain conclusions about what the laity are called to do in the Church and in the world and about how the ordained and the lay ministries in the Church are complementary to each other and together form a partnership.

When the bishops of England and Wales responded to the National Pastoral Congress of 1980 in 'The Easter People' they spoke often of the 'Sharing Church' and declared:

> We should like to see the lay members of our Church, men and women, young and old, become steadily more aware of their true dignity in the people of God and of their daily calling as baptised Christians to evangelise the society in which they live and work . . . For they are not simply delegates of the bishops and clergy, they are Gospel-inspired lay-people, members of the laos (or people) of God, and in their own right missionaries of Christ to the world. (Easter People, 27).

This faithfully expresses the teaching of the Second Vatican Council where, in the Constitution of the Church, the Fathers explained:

> the laity, by their very vocation, seek the kingdom of God by engaging in temporal affairs and by ordering them according to the plan of God. They live in the world, that is, in each and in all of the secular professions and occupations. They live in the ordinary circumstances of family and social life . . . They are called there by God so that by exercising their proper function and being led by the Spirit of the Gospel they can work for the sanctification of the world from within, in the manner of leaven. (LG. 31).

The primary and distinctive responsibility of laymen and laywomen then, is to build the kingdom of God in the secular city. This is the laity's missionary vocation; it is one that they usually fulfil in their individual situations and in an individual way. It is a universal vocation addressed to all lay people wherever they are and whatever secular role they have. Have the laity then no responsibility within the Church? The Decree on the Laity and the new Code of Canon Law teach instead that the local church relies on the active involvement of lay people.

> The laity should accustom themselves to working in the parish in close union with their priests, bringing to the Church community their own and the world's problems as well as the questions concerning human salvation, all of which should be examined and resolved by common deliberation. As far as possible the laity ought to collaborate energetically in every apostolic and missionary undertaking sponsored by their local parish. (Decree on Laity, N.10).

The same decree takes it for granted that the laity will help to reclaim the lapsed, to teach the word of God 'by means of catechetical instruction' and 'to offer their special skills to make the care of souls and the administration of the temporalities of the Church more efficient' (ibid.). This constitutes a second and a different level of action for the lay person in the Church. It is the level of voluntary, apostolic action which will normally be the contribution of an active minority. The third level of lay action within the Church would be the undertaking, either on a full-time or part-time basis, of specific ministries, lector, acolyte, catechist, marriage counsellor, pastoral assistant. This I have already discussed.

The new Code of Canon Law takes it for granted that the laity will play an active and responsible part in any local parish or diocese. It recommends the establishment of pastoral councils in each diocese 'to study and weigh those matters which concern the pastoral works in the diocese and to propose practical conclusions concerning them' (Canon 511). Parish priests are asked to ensure that the faithful are concerned for the future of the parish, that they feel themselves to be members both of the diocese and of the universal Church, and that they take part in and sustain works which promote this community (Canon 529 s2). After due consultation, pastoral councils can be set up in a parish so that the laity can 'give their help in fostering pastoral action' (Canon 536). Finance committees can also be established 'to help the parish priest in administration of the goods of the parish' (Canon 537).

The Code also speaks of the primary and universal ministry of the laity and of its more particular forms. Their primary responsibility, declares Canon 225, is 'to strive so that the divine message of salvation may be known and accepted by all people throughout the world'. The laity have the special obligation 'to permeate and perfect the temporal order of things with the spirit of the Gospel'. The Code emphasises the responsibility of married people especially for the Christian formation of their children (Canon 226). But it then goes on to say that laymen can undertake 'the stable ministry of lector and acolyte' or, and this is significant, the laity can be given 'a temporary assignment to the role of lector in liturgical actions' (Canon 230). This idea of a temporary assignment is one which can and should be further developed and I have elsewhere attempted to do this.

The second point I want to make is about the exercise of co-responsibility in the local church. I am well aware of the tensions and frustrations often experienced in parishes and dioceses. I know that many lay people find it hard to accept being excluded from decision-taking. They point out that they are expected to exercise initiative and responsibility in their vocation as laity in the secular world and are denied such opportunities in their own parishes. At the same time when structures of consultation are established they often run into problems because the laity bring to them their secular experience gained from politics, trade unions or board rooms. If the sharing Church is to become a reality we have to breathe new life into our structures and bring to the conduct of its business new attitudes derived authentically from Gospel and kingdom values.

We can learn something perhaps from the past history of monastic communities. They arose in the Church of western Europe outside the normal ecclesiastical structures. They were the basic communities of the early and late Middle Ages. I am not proposing the monastic model as the prototype in every respect for today's basic communities and local churches. Yet these latter could usefully learn much from the monastic tradition.

Monasticism can make a special and well-tried contribution to the art of community living and the exercise of authority. Let me say at once that I am speaking about the ideal in both cases, realising that success depends on vigilance and hard work on the part of all concerned. Institutional structures do not resolve all human problems. The ideal is rarely, if ever, realised.

I do not propose to dwell on the art of community living. Much has been written on that subject in recent years. I wish rather to speak about the exercise of authority in the monastic community. What I say about monastic chapters can be applied to the parish community, meeting in parish council or assembly. The parallel is not exact but it is suggestive.

In the monastery there is a carefully worked-out balance between the authority of the abbot and the responsibility of the community. St Benedict required the abbot to consult with his community either through the calling of all the brethren to chapter or through a smaller body, the abbot's council. Subsequent monastic constitutions, based on the spirit and letter of the Rule, have developed this fundamental characteristic of monastic policy. The abbot is required to obtain permission from the chapter for certain important actions, for others he needs to consult only. Thus the community has some share in the making of decisions and that sharing can indeed be, at times, decisive. The power of the abbot is thus limited by this requirement to consult; it is also limited by the constant reminders made by St Benedict that the abbot must remember to whom he must render the account for his stewardship. This is more effective than meditating on Lord Acton's dictum: 'Power tends to corrupt and absolute power corrupts absolutely.'

One final point on this monastic model. There are two chapters in the Rule of St Benedict which instruct the abbot on how to carry out his task. These chapters are extraordinarily contemporary; indeed leaders in any walk of life would benefit from a study of them. I do not exclude bishops, busy parish priests or lay leaders.

My third point has to do with the development of lay ministries and co-responsibility within the local community. Every baptised Christian brings the presence and the truth of Christ to every place of work, each social setting, each home, every form of leisure. This is, we all agree, by virtue of baptism and confirmation and it is a mission inspired and nourished by the Eucharist of the local community. This is the sanctification and the transformation from within of the secular reality. There are other forms of ministry already provided throughout the universal Church. It would be a positive development if the local church, in council, were to identify areas of need, to agree on suitable candidates and to commission them in the name of the community for a stated period of time to meet those needs.

I am conscious that in some continents such modest, fore-seeable developments might seem inadequate when measured against what has already happened and what needs to be done. But whatever is further advocated and undertaken must be consistent with our heritage and in union with the universal Church. Growth is always slow, sometimes imperceptible. When a community is in process of growth it is always important to spend time first in genuine consultation and dialogue and to move forward as far as possible with the agreement and support of the community. Yet ultimately when a decision has been properly taken by legitimate authority it is the responsibility of all to accept and promote it.

12
One World Made Holy

The signs are all about us. It does not need a prophet to see that the world is entering a new age where appalling destruction and unparalleled development are the stark alternatives. The technological revolution is gathering momentum. In the hands of the blind, the deaf or the immature, disaster would be the inevitable outcome. There is little time left for the human family to grow to moral maturity. We have to become increasingly conscious that we are a single species in a global village whose finite resources have to be intelligently and responsibly husbanded. We have the capacity to destroy ourselves or each other or the environment but that has to be averted at all costs.

In this endeavour those whose lives are guided by religious belief and principles have an irreplaceable contribution to make. It is highly significant that the renewal of the Catholic Church is taking place at this time and in this context and that the worldwide movement towards Christian unity is helping to fashion a single witness and a concerted contribution from Christians. Together we are called to fulfil the mission of Christ himself that the world might have life and have it more abundantly.

The truth and relevance of what I am saying depends ultimately on how one regards religion and the role of the Church in the affairs of our planet. There are those who resent and reject any involvement of the Church in public affairs. For them religion is exclusively a private concern of each individual. It has to do with personal morality and values; it has a role in regulating relationships; it should be principally concerned with worship, the soul, spiritual things and eternal life. The public and private spheres are strictly demarcated and everything in the world of politics, economics and international relations is thought to be best guided by enlightened self-interest, market forces or considerations of national interest and security.

The Church has always resisted such dualism. John XXIII put the case clearly in his encyclical letter of May 15th, 1961, Mater et Magistra. He opened the argument by saying:

> Christianity is the meeting point of earth and heaven. It lays claim to the whole man, body and soul, intellect and will, inducing him to raise his mind above the changing conditions of this earthly existence and reach upwards for the eternal life of heaven, where one day he will find his unfailing happiness and peace. Hence, though the Church's first care must be for souls, how she can sanctify them and make them share in the gifts of heaven, she concerns herself too with the exigencies of man's daily life, with his livelihood and education and his general temporal welfare and prosperity. (Mater et Magistra, 2–3)

The Second Vatican Council steering the Church along paths of dialogue, discernment and collaboration, was also unambiguous:

> Christ, to be sure, gave his Church no proper mission in the political, economic or social order. The purpose which he set before her is a religious one. But out of this religious mission itself came a function, a light and an energy which can serve to structure and consolidate the human community according to divine law. As a matter of fact, when circumstances of time and place produce the need, she can and indeed should initiate activities on behalf of all men, especially those designed for the needy, such as the works of mercy and similar undertakings. (Gaudium et Spes, 42.1)

The legitimate concern of the Church persists to the present day. When Pope John Paul II published in 1988 his most recent encyclical on social concern he wrote:

> The Church will know that *no temporal achievement* is to be identified with the kingdom of God but that all such achievements simply *reflect* and in a sense *anticipate* the glory of the kingdom, the kingdom which we await at the end of history, when the Lord will come again. But that expectation can never be an excuse for lack of concern for people in their concrete personal situations and in their social, national and international life since the former is conditioned by the latter especially today. (Sollicitudo Rei Socialis, N.48)

The Church can never accept that religion is meant to be entirely private. Our basic personal faith has public consequences. We believe, with the whole Church, that every human being is made in the image and likeness of God and is destined to be his living temple. Therefore each individual possesses a dignity, a value and a freedom which can never be taken away. Whenever the rights and the freedom of the individual are threatened or assailed, Christians and the Church authorities must intervene and act with all possible effectiveness. We believe too that as children of the one God we are one family with mutual responsibility for each other. We must therefore, individually and corporately, have a concern for racial equality, community relations, the rights of immigrants and the often desperate needs of the Third World. And we treasure human life as God's most precious gift and seek to defend and enhance it. We have urgent concerns therefore for issues of war and peace and a deep conscientious abhorrence of abortion and of the new medical and scientific interventions into the process of human conception, procreation and development.

We dare not retreat into a state of spiritualised individualism. The New Testament is full of texts which urge us to respond to the needs of our neighbours. Our Lord left us stories like Dives and Lazarus, the Good Samaritan on the road to Jericho and the account of Judgment Day when our destiny and worth is decided by how we have treated Christ in the person of the hungry, the thirsty, the naked, the stranger, the sick and the imprisoned. St John questioned: 'If a man who was rich enough in this world's goods saw that one of his brothers was in need, but closed his heart to him, how could the love of God be living in him?' (1 John 3:17).

Many critics of the Church's involvement in social concerns would never dream of denying the beauty and relevance of these teachings but would argue that they inculcate individual charity given without a critical stance towards the situation that produced the hardship. The Church, however, has come to realise over the centuries that individual compassion and generosity can never meet the needs of the suffering world. It is not sufficient simply to react to emergencies but to seek where possible to identify the root cause of the problem, to tackle it and to try to ensure it does not recur. Society should learn to accept corporate responsibility and to fashion where necessary structural reforms. This is true of national and international problems. It is part of our growth in community awareness and then in cosmic consciousness. Pope Paul VI argued in his charter for development: 'Development demands bold transformations, innovations that go deep. Urgent reforms should be undertaken without delay' (Populorum Progressio, N.32).

Successive popes have continued to argue that these social questions involve profound moral issues reaching to the heart of our relationship with God, his creation and other people. They can involve personal and corporate sin. Pope John Paul tackles the matter directly in his latest encyclical:

If the present situation can be attributed to difficulties of various kinds, it is not out of place to speak of 'structures of sin' which . . . are rooted in personal sin and thus always linked to the concrete acts of individuals who introduce those structures, consolidate them and make them difficult to remove. And thus they grow stronger, spread and become the source of other sins and so influence people's behaviour.

'Sin' and 'structures of sin' are categories which are

seldom applied to the situation of the contemporary world. However, one cannot easily give a profound understanding of the reality that confronts us unless we give a name to the root of the evils which affect us.

One can certainly speak of 'selfishness' and of 'short-sightedness', of 'mistaken political calculations' and 'imprudent economic decisions'. And in each of these evaluations one hears an echo of an ethical and moral nature. Man's condition is such that a more profound analysis of individual's actions and omissions cannot be achieved without implying, in one way or another, judgements or references of an ethical nature. (Sollicitudo Rei Socialis, N.36).

Since so many social issues are matters of morality, at the very least one must continue to uphold the Church's role as the conscience of international and national society. Detailed technical solutions are not to be found directly in God's revelation but fundamental attitudes decisive in the formulation of such solutions most decidedly are. But not everyone agrees.

It is possible to detect a common strand in all attempts to deny and limit the Church's involvement in public affairs. It is a position explicitly or implicitly endorsed by some members of the Church who have not fully understood her teaching. It fails to recognise the unity and inherent goodness of all created things. It has features in common with an ancient heresy that stems from the life and teaching of Mani, or Manicheus, a third-century Persian. It is well known that for a time St Augustine came under the influence of this teaching and some argue that he never fully escaped from its influence.

Christopher Derrick in his book *The Delicate Creation* summed up the specific and enduring appeal of Manichaeanism:

It makes simple rough sense out of our human condition; it does justice to the mixed character of our experience in this life, to our nostalgic sense of exile and our instinctive equation of the 'spiritual' with the good; and with fair success it attempts to bypass the problem of evil, which must always remain a stumbling block for Christians. (p. 50)

In this dualism the goodness of God is not denied; God remains remote, utterly perfect and impassible, beyond all our knowing. There is, however, a gulf set between the good and loving Father and the evil creator of matter who made this bad, material universe. Light and darkness are locked in perpetual conflict. This world reveals nothing of God's nature or goodness.

I am not claiming that explicit Manichaeanism persists but I am convinced that an underlying and unconscious dualism colours much thinking about the world, our place in it and the role of the Church. It sees little or no religious significance in material things or experience except as distraction to be resisted or an encumbrance to be shed in an upward journey of spiritual self-denial and purification. It is other-worldly and concentrates its efforts on achieving absolute fulfilment in another and eternal life. It sees this life only in terms of preparation for the next and regards it at best as a temporary trial or test.

The trouble, as all Christians would recognise, is that there is here some truth mixed in with the error. It provides one kind of explanation for much that is valid in Christian thinking and experience. But it is ultimately misleading and sterile because based on a vision of reality alien to biblical revelation and the incarnation. Those revealed truths lead us into a deeper understanding of what it means to be Church and to a clearer appreciation of our mission in, and to, the world. It is no new revelation; it springs from the very roots of the Judaeo-Christian tradition.

In that tradition there is but one creation. All that exists is a single outpouring of life and love from the God who freely chooses to share his goodness with his creatures. We find in the book of Genesis at least three fundamental religious truths about creation. It is affirmed first that creation is good and belongs to God. That affirmation in itself is enough to dispel any notion of dualism. It is the foundation of all genuine religious response to material things, to the totality of creation. The created world is never to be dismissed as irrelevant to life's purpose or at odds with human destiny. It is not, in itself, either distracting or dangerous despite human frailty and selfishness. Rather all things are part of God's expression of himself and are his word to us.

Gradually throughout history the implications of this fundamental truth are being realised. At times some religious people have failed to follow through the intellectual consequences of this belief about the divine origin of creation and have shown reluctance to support the endeavours of science and scholarship to explore the physical universe, its formation and subsequent history. Yet it is fundamental to the true Judaeo-Christian tradition to regard all reality as one and God-given and therefore to rule out the possibility of contradictory truths. Science and religion are not in conflict. The new physics and the explosion of astronomic knowledge in fact lead humanity into an inward and outward exploration of reality whose conclusions can only as yet be glimpsed but which appear most stimulating.

It has to be admitted that only gradually have popular misconceptions about the created universe given way to new knowledge and understanding. We were once all 'flat-earthers'; it then took time to come to terms with the idea that the earth rotated around the sun and not vice versa; only in our own days has the scale of creation become apparent. New questions are now being asked of faith when our sun is known to be just one star in a galaxy of 100,000 million other stars and our galaxy one of a hundred billion others. Creation on such a prodigal and as yet inexplicable scale stuns the imagination but has to be understood as an integral whole, as loving in design and conception and as coming from God. The issue is now the centrality of the human race in God's plan for his creation and the significance of the incarnation for what may be other forms of intelligent life in this unimaginable cosmos. Faith answers firmly that the Word of God made flesh in Jesus Christ provides answers, life and love for other, as yet unexplored, worlds. Reality even if not yet dreamed of by us has been from all eternity in the mind of God and will be no more than further revelation of that same infinity. Like our presently known universe it will be a sign of God's loving intent in our regard.

Secondly the Judaeo-Christian understanding of creation leads to the conclusion that the human race has been given by God a unique role in relation to all living things. All the images of the Book of Genesis emphasise however that Adam and Eve, fashioned from the earth, have a common origin with all created reality. Hence interdependence will modify and interpret the seeming mastery given to humanity over the rest of creation. The Judeao–Christian tradition, with its stress on the goodness of creation, portrays human beings as stewards of creation, trusted by God to apply intelligence and skill to the use of the resources of the good earth. They were 'lords of creation' but not tyrants, and not even absolute monarchs since they answered to God for their time on earth. Fallen man has undoubtedly misused his power and squandered finite resources. Frequently his attitude to nature has been exploitive, selfish and shortsighted. Today we face many of the consequences of such an approach. In recent times issues of population, development and ecology have assumed increasing importance and require of today's Church an unambiguous and sensitive response.

It was disheartening to note the apparent indifference of world governments to the 1980 Report of the independent commission on international development issues under the chairmanship of Willy Brandt. That document, the result of careful analysis by respected world leaders, made a powerful case for enlightened self-interest in promoting development and for a recognition of our interdependence. It can help shape new attitudes. The Church is uniquely placed to witness to the unity of the human family and to human responsibility in God's scheme of things for the stewardship of all creation.

I would add that the role of the Church in this regard, although presently urgent, will assume even more importance in the next phase of human affairs when mankind ventures further into the newly discovered cosmos now being tentatively explored by the first space-probes and orbiting space stations. This too is God's creation. What will be mankind's relationship to it and what is our responsibility? What does it mean to be Church not only on this planet but throughout the whole of God's creation?

The third fundamental truth to which the Book of Genesis bears witness is that human beings enjoy a unique relationship to God the Creator. Although all created things are good and please God and reflect his truth, goodness and beauty, human beings are explicitly stated to be made in God's own image and likeness. That special relationship is emphasised not only by the entrusting of created things to human stewardship but by the intimacy and friendship between God and man symbolised by God's walking in the Garden in the cool of the day. From the beginning human intelligence and will, knowledge and love, are seen as something spiritual, as Godlike. Mankind's refusal to obey plunged creation itself into turmoil and caused disruption, darkness and death. God's unswerving love was made manifest in Christ who became not only 'our peace' but the first-fruits and model of the new humanity recreated by God through the Holy Spirit.

Throughout the whole of past history and forward into the future, the human family is called to be one in Christ and to manifest in creation the presence and the power of God's life and love. When the whole of creation is caught up into a single symphony of love, the kingdom of God will have reached fulfilment and God will be all in all. Until that ultimate realisation, the Church brings into unity those who in Christ have come to a new life of absolute love and a new vision of reality. Believers are committed to the building of a new city for mankind, a civilisation of love. So far our understanding has been terrestrial, limited by our understanding of the creation of which we are part. Our belief in the uniqueness of Christ as Son of God would argue for our own uniqueness in the cosmos. But we can, as yet, do no more than wait in faith and hope as the greatness of our mission and destiny is gradually revealed. Perhaps we are the only intelligent life in the cosmos and alone we are called to union with God.

What is increasingly clear however is the scale of our immediate mission and ministry as Church in today's world and on our planet. It is supremely ironic that as we stand on the threshold of a new era and of new worlds we should have in our hands the power to poison the environment of our planet, annihilate our race or at least destroy its potential for peaceful development and progress and thus damage the cosmos as well. Here the Church fulfils its role as 'the universal sacrament of salvation', with a part to play in our world and in the universe.

The two spheres of action are irretrievably linked, as the Council prophetically indicated:

> The Church, to which we are all called in Christ Jesus, and in which by the grace of God we acquire holiness, will receive its perfection only in heaven, when will come the renewal of all things (Acts 3:21). At that time, together with the human race, the universe itself, which is so closely related to man and which attains its destiny through him, will be perfectly re-established in Christ. (LG. 48)

But before new heavens are established, what can the Church do to help develop a new earth?

It is without question the task of the Church and its individual members to call peoples everywhere to a realisation of the fundamental unity, dignity and interdependence of the whole human family. The gradual development of a sense of our human solidarity is essential for our survival and the continuing existence of our planet. We have made progress from family, tribal, regional and national perspectives and loyalties to a growing realisation that we belong to wider communities and ultimately to a worldwide family. Rooted as we are in our own situation, our horizons must embrace the whole world.

States are still intent on fostering the myths of a bygone age and ignoring the truth that planetary self-interest and an awareness of our global interdependence are necessary not only for our future prosperity but for our continued survival. In the light of all the possibilities and dangers our planet faces, it is for the Church, with its necessarily universalist vision, to help lead the peoples of the world to a new understanding of themselves. The self-knowledge of the Church as communio or koinonia has immediate implications for the world of human endeavour. The concept of one people of God inspires us to work for the development of a human family united in its search for the good life. Consequently in promoting the ideal of one world, the Church must be energetic and resolute in its advocacy of racial equality and be ranged against any discrimination based on sex, colour, class or creed.

But there is more. If our planet is to survive we must teach people to walk the ways of peace. In 1982 during his pastoral visit to Britain, Pope John Paul declared at Coventry on Pentecost Sunday: 'Today the scale and the horror of modern warfare – whether nuclear or not – makes it totally unacceptable as a means of settling differences between nations. War should belong to the tragic past, to history; it should find no place on humanity's agenda for the future.'

We should, as Church in today's world, stand uncompromisingly for the sanctity of all innocent human life. It is a value on which our future civilisation must be based. Even the unjust aggressor should be met by the minimum force necessary to deter and restrain. We should devote as much effort to rooting out causes of conflict as to preparing for war. This would require a massive rethinking and redirection of resources.

I am depressed by the huge gap thought appropriate by governments between military expenditure and development expenditure. In Britain defence spending outstrips development aid almost eighteen times. Worldwide military expenditure in 1985 topped £500 billion, almost a million pounds a minute. Five hours of world military spending on that scale is equivalent to UNICEF's total annual budget. One day's expenditure would be the cost of wiping out malaria in a single year. I can find no better witness to cite than General Dwight D. Eisenhower who once said: 'Every gun that is made, every warship launched, every rocket fired, signifies in a final sense a theft from those who hunger and are not fed.'

The Church's official position was clearly set out over a decade ago in a statement to the United Nations by the Holy See:

The obvious contradiction between the waste involved in over production of military devices and the extent of unsatisfied vital needs in the world . . . is in itself an act of aggression . . . which amounts to a crime. For even when armaments are not used, by their cost alone, they kill the poor by causing them to starve. (*Vatican on the Arms Trade*, UN, 1975)

Pope Paul VI's key insight in 1967 was: 'development is the new name for peace'. In other words, unless the poor of the Third World are able to provide the basic necessities of life – food, clothing, shelter, health and education – for themselves and their families, there is little hope that global unrest, and even widespread warfare, can be averted. Perhaps Pope Paul VI's slogan needs to be rewritten as 'peace is the new name for development'. The world community can continue to pursue the arms race and build ever larger arsenals of deadly weapons or it can adopt a totally new set of priorities and move deliberately and urgently towards the provision of basic needs for our global family. It cannot do both. Either we invest in arms and death or we invest in life and the future development of all the peoples of our one world.

Pope John Paul II has again recently insisted that issues of peace and the development of the whole person and the full achievement of both depends on our fidelity to our vocation as men and women of faith. It depends above all on God. The Pope writes:

We are all called, indeed obliged, to face the tremendous challenge of the last decade of the second Millennium, also because the present dangers threaten everyone: a world economic crisis, a war without frontiers, without winners or losers. In the face of such a threat, the distinction between rich individuals and countries will have little value, except that a greater responsibility rests on those who have more and can do more.

This is not however the sole motive or even the most important. At stake is the dignity of the human person whose defence and promotion have been entrusted to us by the Creator . . . As many people are already more or less clearly aware, the present situation does not seem to correspond to this dignity. Every individual is called upon to play his or her part in this peaceful campaign to be conducted by peaceful means, in order to secure development in peace, in order to safeguard nature itself and the world about us. The Church too feels profoundly involved in this enterprise and she hopes for its ultimate success. (Sollicitudo Rei Socialis, N.47)

There is some danger that faced with the international problems of today's world we might be tempted to think that national and local issues are losing their significance and urgency. What it does mean, however, and this is part of the new understanding of the Church's relationship with the whole of life, is that all created things form a single unity and that all are dependent upon God and are interdependent on each other. The consequence is that nothing can, or should, ever be considered in isolation. Local and national industrial problems, economic success and failure, shortage of adequate housing, unemployment or underemployment depend more and more, as Pope John Paul II explicitly recognises, 'on the influence of factors beyond regional boundaries and national frontiers' (Sollicitudo Rei Socialis, N.9). In every sphere of activity there is increasingly apparent a growth in human solidarity, a practical acknowledgment of the ancient insight that 'no man is an island'. And here too the Church has a role.

Christians recognise the unity of all things and their inherent goodness despite the effects of human waywardness and sin. They also see God's presence everywhere, manifesting itself even in unlikely places and people. The Church is not a lone force in the building of God's kingdom on earth but makes a unique contribution to a world where many forces operate for the education, healing and developing of the world's peoples. But at all times the Church is uniquely sustained by Christian hope and a sense that God's kingdom is coming in all the circumstances of life.

The kingdom of God is made real and effective in the person of God made man, our Lord Jesus Christ. He is redeemed humanity. He is the kingdom. We are all called to become one with him, to share divine life, to be part of the kingdom on earth. That kingdom, we are assured, exists now in the last days in mystery, sign and sacrament. It is made present above all in the Lord's own presence and sacrifice in the offering of the Mass which we the baptised are invited to make our own. In the most intimate communion with him we are lifted up in one perfect sacrifice to the Father and are made partakers of God's life and love in and through Christ. In that sense and in that way the kingdom is made present and operative in us.

But there is more. We are not alone; we in each Eucharist are not only united with all the living and dead and the generations still unborn but we proclaim, as stewards of God's creation, the essential unity of that creation. The presence of the risen Lord, the reality of his sacrifice, is made sacramentally possible through the offering of bread and wine, fruit of the earth and work of human hands. These created things are transformed into the body and blood of Jesus Christ in whose person the kingdom is made present. In and through those material gifts, all created nature is offered back to God with us and receives blessing, transformation and new meaning.

The kingdom of God is present now; at the same time it is a future reality. It is internal to the hearts and minds of the baptised; at the same time it is an external reality in the world. In a unique way it is signified and realised in each Eucharist. But the reality is not confined to the liturgical celebration. That has to be seen as the source of divine energy and life in creation. Those who share fully, actively and consciously in the Mass go out into a world awaiting, albeit unknowing, its call to new life. They, then, as Church in the world, help to channel and communicate new life, to heal the damage of sin and to bring people to conversion and an awareness of their need for God and his love for them. In that way the new Jerusalem is built up out of living stones into a new civilisation of love.

As Pope John Paul teaches:

All of us who take part in the Eucharist are called to discover, through this Sacrament, the profound meaning of our actions in the world in favour of development and peace; and to receive from it the strength to commit ourselves ever more generously, following the example of Christ who in this sacrament lays down his life for his friends [cf John 15:13]. Our personal commitment, like Christ's and in union with his, will not be in vain but certainly fruitful. (Sollicitudo Rei Socialis, N.48)

In the Eucharist, which is summit and source of all our life in Christ's body, the scattered human race is gathered together and all creation is bound with it into a single offering to the Father of all that is. One world is thus made holy and given back to God. It is a foretaste and promise of the everlasting banquet in the eternal kingdom.